TEACHING IN JAPAN • ASIA

FINDING THE BEST JOBS

EVERYTHING YOU NEED

TO KNOW TO MOVE

TO ASIA AND GET A

HIGH-PAYING

REWARDING JOB

DOUGLAS MCNAMEE

EAST ASIA PRESS
Seattle, Washington

FIRST EDITION
June 1993

ISBN 0 - 9635678 - 0 2

Edited by Jonathon Takeo Pearson

Cover by Doug Smith

Published by:
East Asia Press
1715 NE Naomi Pl.
Seattle WA 98115
(206) 525-3646

Copyright © 1993 Douglas McNamee.
All rights reserved. No part of this publication
may be reproduced in any form or by any means
without prior permission of the author

Printed in the United States

Acknowledgements

United States

Jonathon Pearson, Douglas Smith, Ron Stein, Ya-Wen Chuang, the Experimental College at the University of Washington

Japan

Dr. Masahiko and Sanae Tarutani, Masafumi Endo, Dr. Hisakazu Isogai, the Uchiyama family, Yasuko Inaba, Toyohiko Kondo, the teachers and students of Kaijo, Midori Takahara, Universal Language Institute, Professor Oskar Tepper, Miss Suzuki, Miyuki Takahashi

Japan

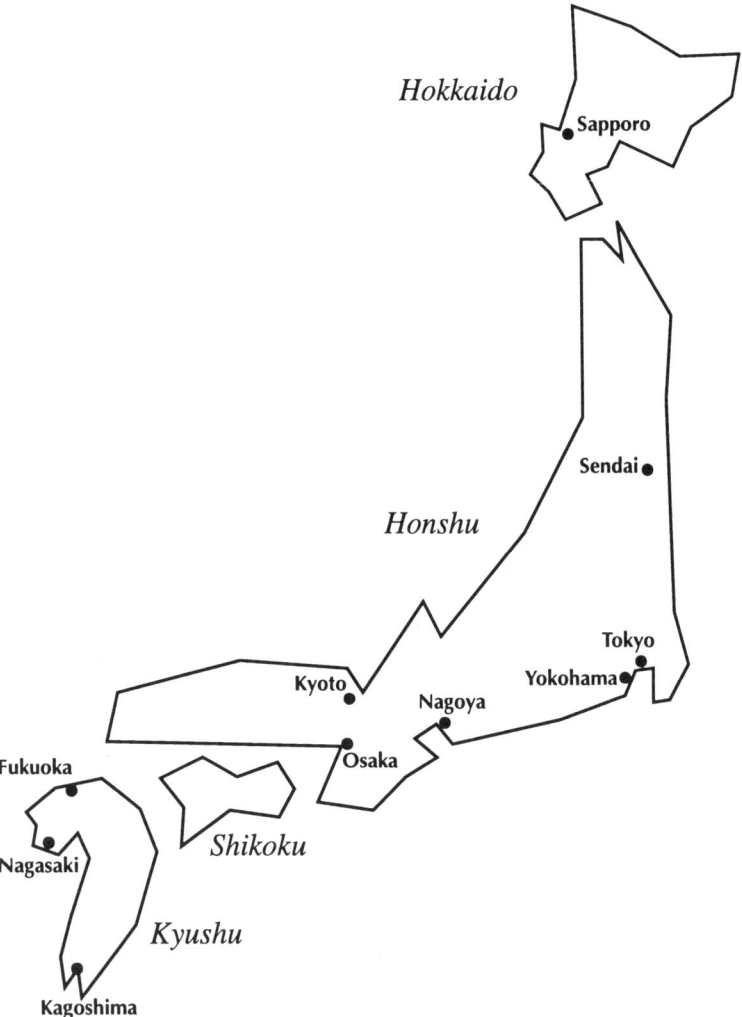

Contents

I. Basics   1
- Introduction
- Why should I live abroad?
- Why Japan?
- Who teaches English?
- English in Japan
- Dispelling the myths

II. Getting a Job Stage 1: Pre-departure   21
- When to go to Japan
- Don't accept a job in your country
- Choosing a destination
- Visas and sponsors
- Long-term preparation
- Just before you go

III. Getting a Job Stage 2: In Japan   41
- Tokyo: the first day
- The different kinds of jobs
- Job components
- Sample work schedules

IV. Getting a Job Stage 3: Specifics   69
- The job search begins
- Job ads in the Monday *Japan Times*
- How to read the ads
- Interviews
- Offers and contracts
- Your obligation
- Immigration

V. Living in Japan — 113
- Apartment hunting
- Phone service
- Cash management
- Health care
- Learning Japanese
- Preparing mentally and culture shock

VI. Teaching English — 139
- Your role as a teacher
- Lesson planning
- Good and bad lessons
- Example lesson
- Teaching adults, students, and children
- Teaching aids and how to use them
- Problems all teachers face

VII. Beyond Teaching — 157
- Forming a long range plan
- Non-teaching jobs
- Working for Japanese companies

Afterword — 161
Appendices — 162
- Recommended reading
- Organizations and information sources
- Budget hotels and inns
- Low cost housing
- Immigration forms
- Useful phone numbers

Index — 183

UNIT 1

BASICS

Introduction

I first went to Japan with no teaching experience and no Japanese language ability. Within three weeks I was employed as a teacher, and after just three months I was teaching at a top-ranked private boys junior high school. In addition to grossing $3,000 a month based on a 25 hour work week, I enjoyed four weeks of paid vacation per year and had unlimited opportunities to teach private lessons at $60.00 an hour. Teaching English in Japan also provided great psychological rewards. I forged strong friendships with people of various nationalities, I learned about Japanese history, society, and economics, and my low working hours and high income allowed me to travel extensively throughout Southeast Asia.

If you are a native English speaker and have a four-year college degree in any subject, you can experience what I did. Assuming that you have a spirit for adventure and a sincere interest in Japan, teaching English can become the vehicle through which your plans to live and work in Asia are finally realized.

Teaching will get you started in Japan. Thereafter, the possibilities for other work or study are almost limitless. While most teachers remain in Japan for 1~2 years, many also stay and work in other fields or pursue scholastic or cultural endeavors. Living in Japan for an extended period will also give you an opportunity to learn Japanese—a language mastered by few Westerners. Furthermore, the friendships you build in Japan will last for life.

From the beginning I would like to emphasize the importance and benefit of going directly to the country you are interested in teaching in and finding work after you arrive. The demand for English teachers has prompted several large schools and organizations to recruit in Western nations, but the salary and benefits that these organizations offer absolutely pale in comparison to what you can find on your own. Although it may seem a bit daunting to simply pack your bags and "go East," I and my friends did it this way and this book will explain how to go about it successfully. As with any endeavor, success depends upon careful planning and foresight. Don't sell yourself short by signing a contract in your country!

Finally, although this book highlights how to find a great teaching job in Japan, its core ideas apply equally to finding teaching work in Taiwan, South Korea, or Southeast Asia. My travel to these areas and discussions with English teachers there indicated that the types of teaching jobs, teaching methodologies, job searching and interviewing, and employment contracts were remarkably similar in nature. Teaching opportunities are most well developed in Japan, but positions in South Korea and Taiwan are rapidly rising. For readers with a strong interest in either of these cultures, employment opportunities are outstanding.

* * *

This book often refers to the United States and Seattle, Washington, as this is the author's home country and city. Of course, not every reader will be American or from Seattle, but this book provides relevant information to anyone anywhere with an interest in living and working in Japan.

How much is ¥2,000 yen in U.S. dollars?

At the time of this writing, the yen~dollar exchange rate stands at ¥105 to one U.S. dollar. Consequently, all financial references in this book are based on this rate. As a general guide:

- ¥1,000 yen = U.S. $ 9.50
- ¥10,000 yen = U.S. $95.00

There are several references to two companies where I worked in Tokyo, but I have changed the names. The first is the Tokyo English Academy (hereafter, TEA), and the Universal Teaching Academy (hereafter, UTA).

Why Should I Live Abroad?

Cultural enrichment

There is so much to see in a foreign country, and no tourist on even a three-week vacation can get more than a cursory view of the people and society. To really learn about a culture you must become a participant in it. Working, paying rent, shopping for groceries, and living in the community will teach you about the way the Japanese people live. Looking at temples and staying in youth hostels is entertaining, but not enlightening. Budget-minded backpack toting travelers often criticize vacationing tourists as people who never get a look at the "real culture," but backpackers hanging out in youth hostels with other foreign travelers are also highly limited in the extent to which they can truly participate in the culture.

Learn about your country and yourself

Living in Japan also gives you an entirely new perspective on your own culture. The U.S. looks quite different from the shadow it casts. Tokyo is a richly international city, and it is almost impossible to avoid contact with people from the U.K., Australia, Canada, China, Korea, New Zealand and elsewhere. You will learn not only what the Japanese think of your country, but what Indians and Malaysians think also. Teaching others will teach you a great deal about yourself. It's challenging and rewarding, and will force you to be creative, learn patience, and develop leadership abilities. The skills I've learned in the classroom have been helpful in countless situations. The chances are also great that you will experience a total reevaluation of your goals while living and working in a foreign country.

Have the time of your life

Perhaps the best part about living abroad is that it's fun and filled with excitement. Every day is an adventure. Even when you are working hard and are short on free time, all you have to do is look around and absorb the collage of neon-lit Chinese characters, the masses of people, and countless examples of starkly conservative and boldly modern architecture, and you will realize that you are doing something truly unique. My first trip felt like a four-year vacation. Looking back, I can't believe it was four years—it went by too fast. In fact, "returning home" was a kind of let down. Conversations with old friends made me quickly realize that while I had been having an adventure abroad, my friends in Seattle were doing the same thing as when I had left! All of my friends and acquaintances that have lived in Asia and returned home all want to go back and live in Asia again.

Overall, living abroad is a lot like going to college. People go for different reasons and get different things out of it. It is a completely new, exciting, and stimulating environment. It exposes you to things you never knew existed. This exposure usually leads to changes in how one sees the world and him/herself. It also usually has a profound effect on one's long-term career plans. Is it easy to get a job in Asia? This is like asking if it is easy to graduate from college. If you consider your options carefully and go for the right reasons, chances are that you will succeed.

Why Japan?

Fascinating history

Japan's written history stretches over two thousand years. While portions of its most modern cities look like the set from the movie *Blade Runner,* respect for tradition and ancient customs runs deep. One of the most fascinating characteristics of contemporary Japan is how successfully traditional culture coexists with modern elements. Although Japan's reputation for borrowing foreign ideas is well known and perhaps over-emphasized, it is nevertheless true that few countries have achieved Japan's balance between old and new. Now is a particularly interesting period in Japan's history as it redefines its place in the world. Living in Japan will allow you to witness its transformation from its old position of "economic super-power only" to that of a fully participating member of the global economy.

Importance of U.S. - Japan relations

Given the close economic, defense, and political ties between America and Japan, it is ironic that Americans have such a pitifully low understanding of Japan. While the average Japanese' knowledge of America encompasses basic history, politics, and society, a recent American college poll revealed that 95% of respondents did not know who Japan's current prime minister is, and a full 40% did not even realize that Japan is an island nation! As Americans learn more about Japan, it is clear that the demand for people knowledgeable about Japan will increase. Time spent in Japan will allow you to become well versed on Japan related topics, and language study will give you greater flexibility in building future career options. Although media sources occasionally make reference to a "Japanese language boom" in Western countries, I know of only a handful of individuals who can actually speak, read, and write the language fluently *and* have a true understanding of Japanese people and customs.

Safety

Japan's enviably low crime rate makes it an extremely safe country to live and work in. Street crime is almost nonexistent, and women walk without fear throughout Tokyo at any time of day. This makes it particularly appealing for women who are intrigued by the adventure of overseas travel but don't want to deal with the constant fear of personal attack. Never in four years in Tokyo did I ever feel the slightest concern for my safety. Moreover, the Japanese penchant for law and order extends to work contracts and apartment rental agreements. While unscrupulous individuals exist in every country, common sense and a reasonably careful approach will virtually guarantee your safety and protection of your best interests.

Proximity to Asia

Japan is an almost ideal jumping-off point for travel throughout Asia. Seoul is a two-hour flight from Tokyo, and Bangkok and Hong Kong are just a bit further. A reasonable work schedule and your high income will make travel opportunities to these exotic destinations possible. During my stay in Japan, I was able to sojourn to South Korea twice and visit Thailand and Malaysia.

Strong economy

Although the global recession has had a profound impact on the Japanese economy, English teachers are still in high demand. If anything, economic difficulties have reinforced to the Japanese the importance of global markets and international business. As the language of world business is predominantly conducted in English, the demand for Japanese skilled in the language is just as great as ever. Recent statistics released by the Ministry of International Trade and Industry (MITI) show that more and more small businesses (defined as those employing less than 50 people) are trying to export. Consequently, your skills as a native English speaking teacher are important.

• • • • • • • •

Who Teaches English?

There is a huge variety of people that teach English in Asia, and the reasons they go are even more numerous. Below are just a few examples of the "Asian English Teacher."

Those interested in a cultural education

Although the diversity of people teaching English in Japan is awesome, one thing they all have in common is a spirit for adventure and a desire to expose themselves to the world. As was highlighted above, *living* in Japan is much more of a cultural experience than traveling there. English teachers work only part-time, so there is plenty of time to get out and absorb your surroundings. As teaching wages are high, those interested in the Japanese language, flower arrangement, kendo, or the tea ceremony will be able to study freely. As you make Japanese friends, they will be eager to take you out, show you places of interest, and invite you into their homes. While living abroad is not for everyone, Japan's high standard of living and the circumstances under which you will be able to find good employment make the transition comparatively easy.

Those interested in financial gain

Teaching English in Japan is immensely profitable not only for teachers, but also for the organizations that hire them. While I worked a moderate schedule and took time to travel and study the culture, many acquaintances went to Japan just to make as much money as possible as quickly as possible. By working 35 hour weeks (*very high* for teaching) and being scrupulous with earnings, many people return home after one year with several thousand dollars.

Four year college degree holders

Japanese immigration law states that to get a working visa, you must have a bachelor's degree. Because of this law, any employer who wishes to get you a working visa will absolutely require that you have a four-year degree. Even if you have lots of teaching experience, it is unlikely that you could even get an interview if you openly admit that you don't have a degree. There are plenty of people teaching in Japan who don't have degrees, but they are also working illegally without a working visa. If you are caught teaching without a proper visa, you may face immediate deportation and will most likely be prohibited from ever entering the country again. Interestingly, your field of study is not important. I successfully taught with a degree in communications, and my other teaching friends had degrees ranging from forest management to political science to microbiology. Although visas will be discussed in later units, know beforehand that you must take official proof of your graduation and degree. "Official proof" includes your diploma (the real thing) or an official document from your school that is signed by the registrar and embossed with the school's seal. Once again, *photocopies are not acceptable forms of proof.*

Educators seeking practical experience

There is a position for almost every kind of teacher in Japan. If your background is education and you are interested in getting practical experience to diversify your degree, you will have limitless employment opportunities. For those just graduating with masters degrees in TEFL (Teaching English as a Foreign Language) or TESOL (Teaching English to Speakers of Other Languages), time spent teaching in Japan will complement your degree by giving you international experience. There are teaching opportunities at private language schools, junior and senior high schools, colleges and universities, and multinational Japanese corporations.

Age

There are no definitive age requirements for English Teachers in Japan. While different schools will look for various kinds of teachers, most of the teachers in Japan are between the ages of 21 to 35. Opportunities exist for people over 40—especially if you have an education background or multinational business experience—but most schools hire younger individuals who are seen as being more modern and familiar with current culture. With regard to age, the critical factor is the type of students in the class. For university student classes, schools will lean toward younger, exuberant teachers. But for a class of mid-level company executives, an older teacher provides an aura of respect and credibility.

Gender

While Japanese fair employment standards allow employers to search for applicants of a specific sex, employers overwhelmingly emphasize attitude and enthusiasm. From my observation, male teachers outnumbered females approximately 3:2, but this is because more males go abroad to teach than females. Most schools appreciate diversity in their teaching staff and thus actively recruit all types of applicants.

Why I went to Japan

My early and frequent contacts with Seattle's large Asian community sparked an interest in oriental cultures, and I thus developed a desire to live and travel in that part of the world. After graduating from the University of Washington, my search for international opportunities lead me to organizations such as the Peace Corps which did not suit my interests. I then met someone who had been to Japan and she told me about the opportunities for teaching. One year later I was in Tokyo, and there I remained for four years. I enjoyed teaching as my main source of income, and my contacts eventually enabled me to land a job as a photographer. I look forward to returning to Japan and Asia in the future, and will remember teaching as the experience that opened me up to Asia.

• • • • • • • •

English in Japan

English study and the Japanese: strange bedfellows

Although junior and senior high schools in America are increasingly making some foreign language study mandatory, the *average* Japanese high school student graduates with 5~7 years of formal English language study. Starting in the first year of junior high, students study English every day until they finish high school. With such an apparently strong commitment to English in the school system, the need for teachers to come from abroad seems ironic if not improbable. Once in Japan, however, what you quickly realize is that native teachers are necessary because of the way in which English is taught. Rather than as a tool for communication and the sharing of ideas, English is broken down into a science and is taught in the same way as calculus or physics. Students are forced to learn arcane rules of grammar that many—if not most—American college graduates are unfamiliar with. The classroom emphasis is on grammar, spelling, composition, and translation. Recent reformers have suggested the importance of developing speaking skills, but only the most progressive and private schools seem to be changing their methodologies. In Japan, it is not at all uncommon that many highly educated Japanese who are teaching English *cannot speak the language.*

Why is English taught in this way?

The main purpose of English classes is to prepare students for the infamously difficult university entrance examinations. These grueling tests are highly competitive and test students over many disciplines including English. Unlike Western university admissions committees which evaluate a combination of national test scores, grade point averages, and extracurricular activities to determine admission for any given candidate, Japanese universities rely almost entirely upon test scores. Since speaking skills are difficult to objectively measure, areas that are easier to quantify are tested. Hence, the university test examination system encourages students to master non-speaking skills. Junior and senior high schools are reluctant to change their curricula as they are in turn judged by their success ratio in placing students at top schools. Many argue that the emphasis on examinations is seriously misguided, but until the system radically changes, the need for native speakers to teach the Japanese how to actually use English will remain high.

What is my role as a teacher?

Native speakers are in demand because they help to fulfill the original reason why most people study language: to communicate through speech. As can be inferred from the discussion above, most educated Japanese have a fairly decent grasp of English fundamentals. Many of my students and Japanese friends who could not even sustain the most rudimentary conversation in English could, on the other hand, read and understand English books and magazines. In fact, one of my best students voraciously read English versions of books by authors Sidney Sheldon and Tom Clancy, but could not even ask me simple questions such as "How old are you?" or "Do you like to sing karaoke?"

Consequently, "English Teacher" is perhaps something of a misnomer as most English teachers in Japan are *not* expected to be grammar experts. Rather than "English Teacher," my other teaching friends and I called ourselves "English Communication Facilitators." To avoid embarrassment, you should certainly refresh your memory of grammar fundamentals in the event that you are asked these kinds of questions, but your skills and enthusiasm as a person who encourages your students to talk will be most appreciated.

Aside from helping the Japanese develop speaking skills, perhaps your second greatest role will be that of a cultural ambassador. You will be the first foreigner that most of your students will have extensive contact with, and they will thus be interested in learning about where you are from and what your impressions of Japan are. Their impressions of the West, in turn, will be largely shaped by their encounters with you.

Why is English study so popular?

Japan's 123.5 million people living on an island chain equal in area to the state of Montana is the epitome of the Malthusian nightmare: population has long since overtaken agricultural capacity. While Japan has enjoyed unprecedented economic prosperity, it also realizes that its success is tenuous and that it is reliant upon global trade and exchange. As the language of international business is English, an ability to effectively communicate is paramount to Japan's success and survival. Furthermore, increasing pressure on Japan to take more of a leadership position in the world demands that the Japanese improve their communication skills. Although it is true that the number of Japanese who will actually *need* to speak English is low, Tokyo's status as an international city and its position as the business and governmental center of Japan constantly spotlights Western nations and English usage. Language schools in Tokyo have very effectively marketed this "need" to learn English—recent estimates indicate that there are over 800 language schools within the greater metropolitan Tokyo area alone! English conversation study is particularly popular with university aged students. People in the 25~35 age group are traveling overseas at historically high rates and are thus fueling a large part of the foreign language boom in Japan. Foreign direct investment mandates that Japanese expatriates be proficient in English and other languages, so corporations also encourage language study. In sum, while the study of other languages is dramatically rising, English is still by far the most popular language to learn.

No rules

English in Japan remains a largely unregulated industry. There is no teacher's union nor a minimum wage. There are no standard qualifications for getting good jobs. One school might hire teachers based on experience and training, while another hires teachers that *"look American."*

To get the most out of your time in Asia, it is essential that you fully understand the job market and all the components that make up the jobs.

● ● ● ● ● ● ● ●

Why Teach English?

High turnover = high demand

Eventually everyone who goes to Japan leaves the country or changes professions. Furthermore, new teaching positions are created every day. As was mentioned earlier, the average English teacher in Japan stays between 1~2 years. After he or she leaves, someone must be hired. The high number of English language schools and steady interest in the language guarantee continued demand for teachers.

No special qualifications necessary

If you are a native English speaker (English is your first language), have a four year degree in any subject, and are sincerely interested in Japan and the Japanese, you can get a rewarding teaching position. Certainly those with masters degrees in TEFL or TESOL will have greater possibilities, but less than 5% of the teachers in Japan have such degrees. Remember, you are hired for your ability to facilitate and encourage conversation in a friendly way—not to teach grammar and sentence structure.

High pay, short hours

The minimum pay for someone new to Japan with no experience or training is ¥2,500 per hour. Most teachers work about 25 hours a week of actual class instruction. While virtually all teachers supplement their main source of income with private lessons, working an average schedule at the lowest wage will still gross $2,000 per month. With approximately 5 hours of private instruction—standard wages are between ¥5,000~10,000 per hour—it is easy to regularly gross $3,000 per month. Are you currently making this amount of money with a thirty hour work week?

Total immersion in the Japanese culture

Teaching gives you immediate access to the Japanese people. On your first working day, you will learn something about your students and their culture. Such opportunities don't exist behind desks or computer terminals.

Be your own boss

This is one of the greatest things about teaching—most employers will let you do whatever you want. During my three years at Kaijo Junior High School, as long as there were no complaints from students or other teachers, I did exactly what I wanted in my classes. I didn't have to submit anything for approval, propose anything, or defend any of my activities or techniques. After a requisite amount of instruction in teaching methods, I was free to be creative in my lesson plans and activities. Since you are serving a paying clientele, as long as they are satisfied your employer will be happy and let you continue to do what you do best.

I am hopeful that this brief overview has convinced you that teaching English in Japan is an excellent way to earn money and learn about another culture. In the event that you still may have some doubts, I have addressed the most common myths about teaching English in the following pages.

● ● ● ● ● ● ● ●

Dispelling the Myths

If teaching in Japan is so easy, lucrative, and interesting, then why don't more people do it? Because most people simply refuse to believe that you don't have to be fluent in Japanese and in possession of a teaching certificate to get a great job. I often hear people say, "I wish I could go to Japan, but...

...I can't speak Japanese."

English conversation is taught *in English*. Furthermore, you will not be teaching the language from scratch—the Japanese study English through junior and senior high school and thereby develop a reasonable grasp of the language. Your lessons will focus on conversational practice through activities that emphasize functional speech. Most classes at private language schools do not even teach writing skills. Finally, language school owners may respect those few foreigners who can speak Japanese, but most will insist that you not use Japanese in your classes. Once students know you can speak Japanese, they will not try as hard to use the target language.

As far as living in Japan is concerned, the abundance of English language services and publications is overwhelming. In fact, a concerted effort to *avoid* English must be made by those trying to learn Japanese. English is, in a word, pervasive: there are four English language newspapers printed daily, bilingual newscasts and other shows imported from America, FEN English radio broadcasts, several English magazines, subway and train information is written in English, and there are many English help lines available to those with immediate problems. It is all too easy to live and prosper in Japan without knowing a word of Japanese. One acquaintance of mine has lived in Japan for twelve years and speaks virtually no Japanese.

...I have no teaching experience or training."

Since you are not really teaching the language and your students will be meeting you, on average, once or twice a week, classes are more of a cultural exchange. Most of the time instructors guide conversations and activities. It doesn't take a teaching certificate to be successful at this. Even with unmotivated students, all it takes is a little determination, enthusiasm, and creativity to get your students excited about English. Although the competition for jobs is slowly raising the minimum qualifications for getting good work, the demand for teachers is such that it is impossible to supply every English class in Japan with a Japanese speaking TEFL expert.

...Japan is too expensive."

Does a cup of coffee really cost five dollars? Who can afford to buy a one hundred dollar melon? All of the outrageous things you've heard about prices in Japan are probably true, but most of these items are things that most Japanese would never buy. Only the fashion conscious and rich frequent Ginza coffee shops where coffee can cost five dollars, and one hundred dollar melons are presents that company presidents may send to their best customers. The average Japanese person gets by just fine on a modest salary, and coffee and fruit can be purchased for extremely reasonable prices. True, if you insist on having a huge apartment and eating beef five nights a week then you may run out of savings quickly, but if you adopt a lifestyle similar to the Japanese, your high salary will allow you to develop considerable savings. Even for those just off the boat with no experience, you can easily find a job that pays $2,250 a month for twenty-five hours a week. An apartment, food, health insurance, entertainment and extras can be had for $1,250 per month. That leaves you $1,000. Are you saving that kind of money now, working part-time at a fun and interesting job?

...I need job and visa before I go to Japan."

The best jobs are found *in Japan*. The only way to get there is on a tourist visa. There is nothing illegal or difficult about looking for work in Japan. Finding and accepting a teaching job in your country and then going to Japan is selling yourself short. Compare the numbers—AEON and GEOS are private language schools that recruit in the U.S. They require long-term commitments and pay less than average wages. Finding work in Japan affords you the privilege of making your own choices. You decide where you will live, who you will teach, and when you will work. You learn about the job market as you go along and you can customize your teaching work to accommodate changes in your life. If you sign a contract in your home country, you will be severely restricted in your ability to make adjustments to your schedule. After securing a job in Japan, your employer will help you get a working visa. Read more about visas and immigration in units 2 and 4.

...the Japanese work too hard."

My impression of the Japanese worker is that he or she spends lots of *time* at work, but is not necessarily working hard! Japanese factory productivity is incredibly high, but salaried workers and office staff did not impress me as being particularly hard-working or efficient. As a foreign teacher, your role is highly defined and the Japanese have no expectation that you will hang out at the office until 8:00 p.m. and then swill beer with co-workers until the last train. Outside of the number of hours you agree to teach in your contract, your only other time at the office will be spent preparing lessons. After you become accustomed to teaching, preparation for a one-hour lesson should not take you more than fifteen minutes.

...the Japanese hate foreigners."

It would be unrealistic to think that one could spend a year in Japan and not have a few negative encounters with some close-minded people. The Japanese have an international reputation for being exclusive and homogeneous in thought, but most inhabitants of larger cities are curious about foreigners and will never display any open hostility. Furthermore, students of English tend to be more liberal minded, internationally acclimated, and generally interested in you. Over a four year period I had a few unpleasant experiences, but I didn't dwell on them. Such encounters are actually quite educational in that they develop your sensitivity to what the minority groups living in your country must feel. Overall, the Japanese are extremely hospitable and go to great lengths to accommodate visitors. If you display sensitivity to their culture, you will be warmly received and welcomed.

UNIT 2

GETTING A JOB STAGE ONE: PRE-DEPARTURE

When to go to Japan

It is best to plan your trip to Japan to coincide with the peak hiring periods in March~April and September~October.

Peak hiring cycles

Language schools hire year round as personnel needs dictate, but there are two hiring peaks: March~April and September~October. While the former period represents the beginning of the academic and business fiscal years, the latter period signifies the end of the summer vacation season. Advertisements for teaching positions in *The Japan Times* reach an all year high during these periods, and it is not uncommon to find 60~80 teaching ads in the Monday edition. Hiring still occurs in other months, but the widest variety of opportunities exist during these two periods. Even though January is a particularly slow month for hiring, in the January 11, 1993 (Monday issue) of *The Japan Times,* there were over 35 advertisements for teaching positions. (Examples of classified ads and how to read them is covered in detail in unit four.)

The Japanese school year

The Japanese academic year begins in April and continues until August when students are given a two-to three-week summer vacation. For those interested in getting positions at schools, most hiring occurs in March, but some additional hiring is done in early September. I taught at a private boys junior high school and a private girls junior high school through my employer. Thus, I was *hired* by *TEA* but I *taught* in the Japanese school system.

Don't Accept a Job in Your Country

While the prospect of securing work and a contract before going to Japan seems comforting, I cannot recommend that anyone do this. Furthermore, the few companies that do recruit in America are ridiculously selective and turn away thousands of qualified applicants each year. Even with my years of teaching experience in Japan, I seriously doubt that any company that recruited me here today would pay me even 60% of the salary I was making through my job which I found myself.

Furthermore, organizations that recruit abroad turn away thousands of otherwise qualified applicants. The well-known *JET Program,* for example, hires approximately 1 out of 40 people it interviews. While signing a contract here may give you a modicum of security, you will give up flexibility to make your own decisions with regard to where you will live, who you will teach, and what your work schedule will be like. More importantly, the pay that organizations such as GEOS and AEON offer is *marginal at best.* Among my friends who were teaching in Japan when I was, only *one person* obtained a job prior to coming to Japan. She, incidentally, broke her contract and found more favorable terms of employment three months after arriving in Japan but had to haggle with her ex-employer and immigration for two months.

The few advantages of signing a contract outside of Japan include the following:

- **Return airfare.** Most companies that hire abroad will pay for your roundtrip airfare *contingent* upon your fulfilling your half of the contract.

- **Visa and sponsorship.** Your working visa and sponsorship will be handled by the company before you go to Japan.

- **Apartment.** Most companies will arrange accommodations for you which saves time and money, but you lose control over location. While it is convenient to have an apartment set up for you, how can you be sure that the accommodations will be to your liking?

Why jobs found in Japan are better

- **Pay.** Salaries are higher for jobs found in Japan. As discussed above, the *minimum* you can expect is ¥250,000 per month based on a 25-hour work week. Companies hiring abroad often pay this same amount for *forty*-hour work weeks.

- **Location.** You get to choose where you will work—the mountains, the country, the seaside, the city, north, south, wherever. Choose a locale that suits you.

- **Options.** You can choose all of the other aspects of your job as well. Interviewing in Japan will enable you to look at the school or company carefully. You should have the freedom to decide between small or large classes, the age of your students, the students' ability level, your teaching schedule, and work load.

- **Contract length.** If you sign in your country, the contract length is often *two years*. It seems risky to agree to anything for two years on a sight unseen basis. Two years is especially long if a "completion bonus" (read: the part of your salary that is withheld as a ransom) is part of your contract.

- **Quitting.** Companies that hire in your country can make it very difficult to quit should you decide that the position is not compatible with your needs. Before you even get on the plane to Japan, the company has you legally and financially by the neck.

Why companies like to hire people in Japan

The size of most language schools is such that going to a Western country to hire three or four teachers is simply not economically feasible. Furthermore, and perhaps most importantly, your independent decision to go to Japan *impresses employers.* Your decision indicates that you are:

- **Motivated to teach**
- **Sincerely interested in Japan**
- **Open to challenges**
- **Adventuresome**
- **Resourceful**

When a company hires a teacher abroad, a staff member often has to pick her up at the airport when she arrives in Japan and then hold her hand throughout the process of adjusting to life in a foreign country. This pampering establishes a bad precedent that most companies don't need to deal with. Why would any company want to put itself in the position of baby-sitter?

People often ask me if they should be sending cover letters and resumes to Japan now, prior to their trip. My answer is no. Unless you are highly qualified or have a personal connection in that organization, they probably won't even keep your resume on file and they definitely will not contact you in the United States. How well you are received by people, how personable you are, and how you present yourself mean everything in Asia. Without a personality to associate your resume with, it is a meaningless piece of paper.

If you have an opportunity to speak with language schools hiring in your country, by all means go and listen to their proposals. Do not, however, let them convince you that it is difficult or illegal for you to go to Japan and get a job yourself. In exchange for having to deal with a short period of uncertainty, you will be rewarded ten times for your patience and foresight. Moreover, initiating and going through with this first stage by yourself is immensely satisfying. After all, isn't one of the reasons why you want to live overseas to build your self-confidence and spirit of adventure?

• • • • • • • •

Choosing a Destination

Although teaching opportunities are available in rural as well as urban areas, you should probably target an urban area until you get experience and get settled in your new country.

Tokyo

I recommend to most people considering teaching in Japan to head for Tokyo first. While the urban blight and overcrowding that Tokyo is known for turns off many foreigners, it is by far the best and easiest place to find teaching work. Even if your ultimate interest is to live in a secluded Japanese hamlet and teach rice farmers English, your interests are best served by starting in Tokyo. Rapid employment possibilities will allow you to start saving money, get teaching experience, and start learning Japanese at a language school. Later, after you have become accustomed to Japan and feel comfortable getting around, look for other job possibilities in more remote regions. If you absolutely do not want to go to Tokyo first, many teaching positions are available in Japan's second largest city, Osaka. Once you are established and accustomed to teaching, your base in Osaka will allow you to investigate teaching opportunities in more remote areas of southwestern Japan.

Tokyo is the only place I've lived in Japan. It's much different from Seattle, which has mountains, lakes, fresh air and a relatively dull night life. This great contrast was one reason I enjoyed living in Tokyo. My Tokyo apartment was about the size of a small bedroom back in the States, but I did not spend lots of time there anyway. I was usually out taking pictures or traveling in Southeast Asia. Being a photographer and guitar player, I was drawn to the art and music scene that thrives in the Japanese capital. Although Kyoto is still arguably the historical and cultural center of the Japan of old, no city in Japan and only a handful internationally can match Tokyo's diversity. People from all over the world come to Tokyo to study and do business. Tokyo provided me with an opportunity to live in Japanese society *and* meet people from many different countries.

Teaching opportunities

With almost twenty million people in the greater Tokyo/Yokohama metropolitan area, there are thousands of teaching opportunities. As mentioned earlier, there are over eight hundred English schools just in greater Tokyo.

Almost all cities seem to have some English conversation courses available to their residents, but the number of teaching positions is drastically less than in Tokyo. Consider the following story:

A friend of mine who was teaching in Tokyo got married and moved to Kumamoto, a large city on the southern island of Kyushu. She had two years teaching experience in Tokyo. She was a skilled teacher and her company did everything they could to keep her from moving. Her husband's work was in Kumamoto and she reasoned that a fair number of teaching opportunities should exist given the city's large population. Within two months she had talked to all of the language schools in the city and had come to know every foreign teacher living in Kumamoto. She exhausted all possible teaching employment sources and yet her search had not been successful. The lesson she learned was that even in "large" cities the number of teaching opportunities pales in comparison to those in Tokyo, and to a lesser extent, Osaka.

It is still quite possible to teach in more remote regions of Japan, but only consider doing so once you have earned some money and gotten experience in Tokyo—and by all means don't move to a small city until you have accepted a job and have signed a contract!

Living conditions

Although most teaching opportunities are definitely in Tokyo, the throngs of people that make this possible also make the living conditions rather cramped. Small apartments with private bath in Tokyo can be easily found for $600 U.S., but the same $600 would get you a three room apartment in the suburbs. The simple rule to remember is that anything within a twenty minute commute of any major station in central Tokyo will be expensive. The further out you go, the lower rents become. Sometimes English schools in small cities will offer a free apartment or house in order to entice talent out of Tokyo.

Learning Japanese

If learning Japanese is one of your reasons for teaching in Japan, try to eventually move to a smaller city. As mentioned above, the ubiquitous nature of English in Tokyo eases the stresses of living for foreigners new to Japan, but this same factor makes learning Japanese difficult. Learning Japanese is not like learning Spanish or any other Indo-European language. It is impossible to just "pick up" the language by watching television commercials and riding packed trains; you must make a concerted effort to use it daily. In smaller cities there are considerably fewer English speaking Japanese, so you will have much greater opportunity to speak Japanese. In fact, your communication survival may depend on it! Your first months spent in Tokyo can get you accustomed to the language, and the many Japanese language schools will enable you to develop a reasonably strong grasp of fundamentals. Then, if you are still interested in learning more, time spent in a remoter area would be an excellent way to continue.

How to find a job outside of Tokyo

In the bigger cities—Osaka, Fukuoka and Sapporo—jobs can be found by going there directly and hitting the streets, checking an English paper's classified section, talking to foreigners working there, and cold calling language schools.

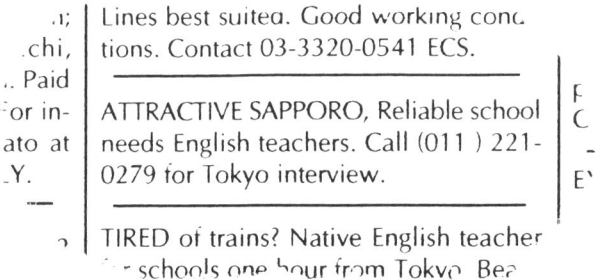

Jobs all over Japan can also be found in Tokyo. If an English school is in a remote place, its staff will have to go to a big city to find good teachers. Often, they place ads in *The Japan Times* and hold interviews in Tokyo. See more examples of these types of advertisements in unit 4.

Summary

Unless you have taught English in Japan before, starting out in Tokyo is your best bet. While opportunities exist all over the country, lots of time and money can be wasted trying to find these. Living in Tokyo will allow you to get teaching experience, save money, learn basic Japanese, and survey prospects in other areas *while you are working*.

Visas and Sponsors

As in any industrialized country, Japanese visa regulations and procedures are complicated and often revised. Between 1986 and 1990, the procedure for changing a tourist visa to a working visa changed three times. Most foreigners in Japan have either a tourist, cultural, *or* working *visa.*

Tourist visas

For American citizens arriving in Japan, passports are stamped and your stay is good for ninety days. Due to reciprocity between Japanese and American immigration authorities, it is not necessary to go to the consulate to get a visa prior to travel. Unless you sign a contract and agree to work for a company hiring in your country, it is impossible to get a working visa before going to Japan. You cannot apply for a working visa without a job first. After three months, the tourist visa is renewable at the immigration office for an additional ninety days. If you want to remain a tourist after 180 days, you must leave the country and come back. Then, you will have a ninety-day tourist visa which can be extended an additional ninety days. Technically, tourists are not supposed to do any kind of work. This means that you have six months to find employment at a company that will help you get a working visa. Some people who teach English do so illegally by renewing their tourist visas several times. While immigration officials are not known to be overly concerned with illegal English teachers, I cannot advise that you work without the proper visa. Getting a working visa is not too difficult, it gives you legal protection, and provides peace of mind.

Sponsors

A sponsor is an individual, usually the owner of the company that hired you, that guarantees to the Japanese authorities that you have a job and a constant income. Part of the requirement of getting a working visa is that a Japanese person agrees to be your legal sponsor. If you cause any trouble in Japan, your sponsor will have to answer for your actions. Thus, sponsorship isn't given out easily. The company will want to know that the person they hired is a responsible, dependable person.

Working visas

This stamp in your passport gives you permission to earn money in Japan. It is good for one year and is renewable an indefinite number of times. There are several different working visa classifications that are defined by category and skill level of work. Examples of working visas include diplomatic, entertainer, professor, research scientist, etc.

Changing from a tourist to a working visa

So there you are, in Japan with your tourist visa, looking for a job. You answer an ad for the New Tokyo English Academy (NTEA). They decide to hire you for twenty-three hours a week and they agree to sponsor you. Most likely, they'll want you to start right away, but visas can't be changed overnight. Paperwork has to be prepared. At immigration, you'll be asked to provide a resume, proof of graduation, a letter stating why you want to teach English, a copy of your work contract with the school, and a few immigration forms. NTEA will help you get your part of the application together. It takes several weeks for the company to complete their paperwork which includes detailed financial reports. Once the application is prepared, you must take this to the local immigration office and get a *Certificate of Eligibility*. After this point, official policy states that working visa applicants must present the *Certificate of Eligibility* to a Japanese consulate in a *foreign country* (for example, South Korea), get the working visa stamped in your passport, and then return to Japan. While neither I nor any of my teaching friends had to have working visas processed overseas between 1987~90, immigration policy beginning in 1991 made this procedure mandatory for all persons interested in getting working visas.

Some fly-by-night language schools don't care whether their teachers have proper visas or not, and while working for these schools may be easy, remember that you have absolutely no recourse in the event of non-payment of services. (If a school employs teachers illegally, then this should tell you something about its business ethics.)

Cultural visas

An alternative to a working visa is a cultural visa. A cultural visa grants permission to stay in Japan to study some part of the Japanese culture such as language, martial arts, or art. You must be registered to study a minimum number of hours per week, usually twenty, at an approved school. The school you choose to study at will act as your sponsor and provide you with the necessary paperwork. Unlike the working visa, "official" immigration policy states that this visa change can be made in Japan. Once your passport is stamped with the cultural visa, you will be allowed to work a limited number of hours (20~25 per week), but in reality no one tracks how many hours you work. Due to the demand for manual laborers in Japan, many Asians are working in Japan on cultural visas by registering for Japanese study at bogus language schools which serve as fronts for the visa application. Getting a cultural visa is easier than getting a working visa, but you must go to school somewhere and tuition costs may be high.

If you are thinking of getting a cultural visa, make sure that your sponsor obtains a *cultural visa* and not a *student visa*. The latter will not allow you to do any kind of work.

Other visas

If you are married to a Japanese national, you are eligible to obtain a spousal visa. For more information, consult your local Japanese consulate or refer to "A Guide to Residence and Registration Procedures in Japan for Foreign Nationals," published by the Japanese Immigration Association.

Warning: visa laws constantly change

Visa laws are reviewed yearly and change frequently. Moreover, the laws are different for different nationalities, and immigration seems to approach each person on a "case by case" basis. Canadians and Australians are eligible for *working holiday visas*. Check with your local Japanese consulate for the latest immigration laws. In Tokyo, call the Immigration Bureau at **(03) 3471-0031**.

● ● ● ● ● ● ● ●

Long-Term Preparation

Educate yourself

The best thing you can do is learn all that you can about Japan. Teaching in Japan has been popular for several years now so it's likely that you will meet someone who has taught English in Japan. Talk to them, get their advice. Check with your local travel agents or community colleges to see if someone offers a seminar or workshop.

Read all you can about the culture. There are hundreds of books that deal with many different aspects of Japan, and in the appendix there is a list of books I have found particularly enjoyable.

If you live in the Puget Sound area, tune in to *Today's Japan* which airs every night at 1:00 a.m. on PBS. This is an excellent English language news program produced by NHK, the Japanese equivalent of PBS. Although the show is produced and broadcast in Japan, it is not possible to view it in Japan unless you purchase a special satellite tuner.

See the appendix for other sources of information on Japan.

Formal training

Many colleges and universities now offer TESL (teaching English as a second language) certificate courses. The number of class hours required and costs for such programs vary with each school. Though it is not required to possess such a certificate to get a job in Japan, it is well worth your time and money. It will not guarantee a higher salary, but it will definitely help you get a job. Additionally, you will be a better teacher. It will save you some of the stress of *"learning on the job"* and your students will appreciate it. Competition for jobs in Japan is beginning to get stiff. When the U.S. economy slows down teachers in Japan think twice about leaving their positions. A weak U.S. job market also encourages more people (including qualified teachers) to look abroad for employment options.

Experience

Any teaching experience you can get before going to Japan would be valuable. Experience will give you an idea of what teaching English is like, and will give you an edge on the competition for jobs once in Japan. Teaching English to Japanese or other Asian students would be ideal, but any group of foreigners that you could work with would be great. While it is difficult to get a paid position as an English teacher in the States without a masters degree, most large cities have literacy outreach programs for which you can volunteer. Perhaps the best way to get some teaching and tutoring experience is to contact the English as a Second Language department of universities and colleges in your area. As an example, the University of Washington's ESL department is always looking for volunteers willing to be conversation partners and to participate in classes. Volunteering will show you what teaching English conversation is like, and will give you exposure to many Asian students. Participating in such a program will give you experience and give you something to feel good about too!

Money

Regardless of how fast you find a job in Japan, you will need some funds for set up expenses. Payday comes once a month, so it could be six to eight weeks before you see any income. I recommend taking at least $2,000, and more if you can. A room can run between ¥1,500 and ¥3,000 per day, and food and train fare will cost at least ¥2,000 per day. Once you get a job, your employer will probably agree to a cash advance and may also help you with initial apartment expenses.

Learn some Japanese

Any Japanese you learn before you go will be useful. Check your local community college's continuing education or university extension programs for part-time Japanese classes. Also, visit the English as a Second Language department at your local college or university and offer to exchange language lessons with Japanese students. Try to get as much exposure to the language as possible. Rent Japanese movie videos, listen to language tapes in your car and walkman, and watch Japanese language programs on t.v.

● ● ● ● ● ● ● ●

Just Before You Go

- **Bank accounts:** Maintain a checking account in your country while you are in Japan. You can send money directly to this account if the need arises, and you will still be able to make payments via personal checks. This is convenient for student loan payments and for anything that you may order by catalog from home.

- **Accommodations:** Make reservations at a youth hostel or inexpensive Japanese inn for your first few weeks in Tokyo. There are many places to stay that are clean, reasonable, and close to job sources. Guidebooks on Tokyo list several choices, but one place that I recommend is the "Kimi Ryokan" which is located in a major sub-center of Tokyo. Next to the Kimi Ryokan is the Kimi Information Center which is a business service where you can make copies, receive telephone and fax messages, and have your mail delivered. Kimi Information Center also has several teaching positions listed and offers help in finding long-term accommodations. More information about Kimi Information Center follows in the section below.

- **Maps and other information:** Contact the Japan National Tourist Organization (JNTO) and request maps of Japan and Tokyo. They will also send you other more generic travel information.

- **Photo album and/or video tape:** Put together a small photo album or video of your life in your home country. Your Japanese friends will be very interested in seeing pictures of your family, your home, your home town, and of yourself at a younger age.

Take some postcards of your city as well and a map of your state.

- **Resume:** Make sure that you take several copies of your resume. What kind of information to include in your resume is discussed in unit 4.

- **References:** Unless they are from someone who is known to your potential employer, references don't carry much weight in Japan.

- **Proof of graduation:** You will need proof that you graduated and have a bachelors degree. You don't have to take your diploma, but you will need an official document from the registrar of your school. Photocopies are *not* acceptable. The letter I ordered from my university states the following:

    September 8, 1986

    To Whom It May Concern:

    This is to verify that Douglas David McNamee graduated from the University of Washington with the degree of Bachelor of Arts (communications) on August 22, 1986.

    The letter must be on official university stationery and be signed with the school's seal and the registrar's stamp. Take several originals; immigration does not return any documents you give them. I also recommend that you take two original copies of your university transcript. I never had to present them, but they may come in handy if you try to get into a different line of work or study at a school.

- **Air ticket:** Call lots of travel agencies and compare prices. Prices vary greatly among agencies, and a four week advance purchase should allow you to get the best price. From Seattle, I have never paid more than $800 for a round trip ticket during the peak seasons. This fare also included a round-trip ticket to Hong Kong, Seoul, or Bangkok from Tokyo. Travel agents call this type of a ticket "Seattle-Seoul return, Tokyo stop-over, six months open." Tickets are "open" for six months or one year. This means that you can make travel arrangements to Seoul and back to the U.S. at anytime within one year. In the example cited, one could fly into Tokyo, work for three months, take a three-day vacation in Seoul, work for three more months, and then return home for two weeks vacation. Once back in America, you can purchase another ticket and repeat the process again. As mentioned above, this type of ticket will add only $100~150 to the price of a round-trip ticket to Tokyo.

- **International driver's license:** Even if you think it is unlikely that you will ever drive in Japan, get an international driver's license anyway. I didn't think that I would ever drive in Japan, but when I moved I needed to rent a small truck to move my belongings. (This was very cheap; ¥5,000 for the day.) To get an international driver's license, call your local office of the Automobile Association of America. IDL's are good for one year and can be renewed by mail. The fee is about $10.00, and you only need to have a valid driver's license to apply.

- **Clothes:** Japan's climate is similar to that of the U.S. East Coast: hot and humid summers and cold and dry winters. A rainy season also makes the months of June to late July rather unpleasant. Consequently, you must have clothes for all kinds of weather. You will be doing more walking and standing than you have ever done in your life, so take comfortable shoes. I often carried my dress shoes in a bag and changed just before I got to an appointment. (By the way, it's a guaranteed riot in

my classroom when a student asks my shoe size—
29 centimeters.) Also, in many buildings students
and teachers must change shoes at the entrance.
Slippers are always supplied, but they are usually
bright green and too small (small slippers are
incredibly painful!). One of my pet peeves about
teaching was wearing an expensive suit that I didn't
want to buy in the first place, and then being told I
had to wear green, vinyl slippers. I eventually
purchased a pair of "indoor shoes" (*uwabaki* in
Japanese). I also bought several pairs of counterfeit,
Korean made, black Reebok tennis shoes and left
these in the shoe boxes of school entranceways. I
think that I had up to five pairs at one point, and I
imagine that some of these are probably still there! At
Kaijo Junior High School where I spent most of my
time (six hours a day, three days a week, all of them
standing) I wore an expensive pair of running shoes
which made the job bearable. Always check to see
what the other teachers (Japanese) are wearing to see
what's acceptable. Once again, take clothes to match
the season of your arrival and sea mail the rest. See
unit 4 for interview and work clothes.

- **Packages to be sent later:** Take a good supply of
daily essentials and hard-to-get items such as special
contact lens solutions, vitamins, deodorants, and
medicines. Take enough clothes with you to match
the season of your arrival, and pack items that you
will want later in boxes and have them shipped after
you have settled. Sea mail is economical for clothing
and books, and your boxes should arrive in three to
four weeks. If you have big feet—larger than U.S.
size 9 for men and size 7 for women— be sure to
buy a good supply of work and casual shoes. Shoes
to fit larger feet are not as difficult to find in Japan as
they once were, but sizes that do not fall within one

standard deviation of the Japanese norm are expensive!

Postscript: How much stuff do you *really* need?

There are two different schools of thought with regard to how much stuff you should take and have sent to Japan:

School A:

You are not a traveler; you will be working and living in Japan. Proponents of this school believe that you should take everything you need to feel comfortable in Japan. Taking or having possessions sent will spare you the expense of having to make these purchases in Japan. Thus, take your mountain bike, computer, skis, and guitar because repurchasing them in Japan will cost a fortune and you shouldn't deprive yourself of your hobbies for one year or more.

School B:

Your stay in Japan is not permanent, and everything you take will have to be brought back or gotten rid of. Proponents of this school are minimalists who insist that "less is better." They feel that part of the purpose of your visit is to experience the Japanese way of life—not transport your culture and hobbies with you. On a more practical note, minimalists realize all too well that most people anywhere accumulate way too much stuff anyway, and that you will end up giving valuable things away at firesale prices when you find out that shipping your things home will cost more than they are worth.

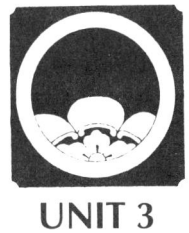

UNIT 3

GETTING A JOB STAGE TWO: IN JAPAN

Tokyo: the First Day

Getting to Tokyo from Narita International Airport

The New Tokyo International Airport (Narita) is not in Tokyo. It is located in Chiba prefecture, 60 minutes by express train from Tokyo. There are three ways to get into Tokyo, but you should budget approximately three hours from when your plane reaches the gate to your destination in Tokyo.

- **NEX:** (Narita Express) is the newest, fastest, most popular, and most expensive ($24) train service to Tokyo and Yokohama. The NEX station is located in the airport terminal. The train leaves about every hour and goes to Tokyo Station, Shinjuku Station, and Yokohama Station. Some trains go directly to Ikebukuro Station. All cars are non-smoking. The ride from Narita to Shinjuku takes approximately 70 minutes.

- **Keisei Skyliner:** Has a station in the airport terminal. Fares are $12 one way and go to Nippori and Ueno Stations in northeast Tokyo. There are 2 non-smoking cars. The ride from Narita to Ueno Station takes approximately 60 minutes.

- **Airport Limousine:** Buses depart from the airport terminal every 20 minutes. Tickets are $21. Destinations in Tokyo typically require 2+ hours depending on traffic. You can choose from several destinations including Shinjuku Station.

- **Taxis:** This is only for those traveling on company expense accounts. One-way fares easily go over $100, and time to Tokyo will be over two hours.

Tourist information

There is a TIC (Tourist Information Center) located in the airport terminal. After coming out of customs you should find it within one minute. Ask for a Tokyo map, a Japan map, a map for any other city or prefecture you are interested in, and a directory of cheap accommodations. If you are confused about anything, ask here. By the way, everyone at TIC will speak English with varying degrees of skill.

Baggage service (takyuubin)

This is a very convenient and reasonably priced service that will deliver your bags or boxes to any location in Tokyo within 1~2 days. Instead of lugging all your things across town for the next couple of hours, have them delivered instead. Cost is about $15 per piece. There are at least 3 companies in the terminal: *ABC* (Airport Baggage Company), *Yamato* (black cat logo), and *Skyporter*. You will need to have an address to send the bags to. Staff members probably do not speak English, but they will try their best to help you. Make sure that your destination address is legible, and printed in Japanese if possible.

Key locations

Upon arrival at Narita Airport, make a stop at the Japan National Tourist Organization's (JNTO) office. There, you can get great maps of Tokyo, general travel information, and other information all for free and in English. The receptionists speak English and will do their best to answer any questions you may have. JNTO has offices throughout Japan, and their Tokyo branch is in Ginza near Yurakucho station.

Prior to arriving in Tokyo, look over a map of Tokyo and familiarize yourself with some of its major features. Because almost all of your travel will be by train or subway, pay particular attention to the station locations and names. One train line, the Yamanote line, circles the city in a continuous loop. The stations on the west side will be particularly important to you as this is where most English schools are located. Traveling by train is not as difficult and confusing as it sounds, and I am sure that you will come to find it incredibly convenient and easy to get accustomed to. All station signs are written in English and Japanese, and with a good map travel anywhere is *easy*.

When you call prospective employers for interviews they will give you directions by train line according to where you are. Have a pen and map handy, and be prepared to write down directions such as "First, take the Yamanote line to Ikebukuro station, and then transfer to the Seibu-Ikebukuro line. Ride the Seibu-Ikebukuro line to the eighth stop, Hoya, and then go out the south exit..." If the school is not near the station, someone may meet you at the station exit.

Kimi Information Center

Your first day should include a trip to the Kimi Information Center in Ikebukuro. Kimi offers services that cater to foreigners, and the staff is bilingual, friendly, and helpful. Kimi has typewriters, copiers, books, job and apartment info, typesetting, fax, bulletin boards, and more. Just down the street they also have a Japanese-style inn, Kimi Ryokan, which offers cheap temporary accommodations. You might consider making reservations to stay at Kimi the first few days. In addition to being close to the information center, Kimi is near Ikebukuro station which has direct train service to Narita airport.

The most valuable service that Kimi offers is a phone answering and mail service. For ¥1,000 per month, Kimi will take your telephone and fax messages and accept your mail. You can call them and get your messages over the phone, and I have found their services to be extremely dependable. If you are staying at a youth hostel, or some other dormitory-type hotel, the operators may not speak English and it will be difficult to get accurate messages. A dependable message service is critical for a successful job search.

Finally, using this service means that you can give your friends, relatives, and creditors a mailing address before you leave for Japan. To establish service, contact Kimi directly at the following address:

Kimi Information Center

KS-7 building 6F, 2-54-3

Toshima-ku, Tokyo Japan, 171

Tel: (03) 3986-1604 Fax: (03) 3986-3037

IKEBUKURO

KS7 Bldg. 6F,
2-54-3 Ikebukuro, Toshima-ku, Tokyo 171

The Different Kinds of Jobs

Teaching jobs fall into eight main categories. Each type is quite different, and you should think hard about which kind of job best suits your personality.

English conversation schools

While the largest English conversation schools, or private language schools, such as ECC and Bilingual often occupy every floor of a building, most schools share space with other companies in large office buildings. The typical school has a small reception area with office space that the director and teachers share and several small classrooms. Class size typically numbers between four to ten students with six students a consistent average.

The clientele of each school will be different, but most schools attract university students and business men and women. Occasionally, junior and senior high school students attend classes. Students at private language schools definitely have widely varying degrees of interest in learning the language. Although some study diligently, the majority treat English study as a fun hobby and come to class to interact with a foreigner, meet others, and learn some English. While many schools sell package lessons spanning anywhere from six to twelve weeks, other schools sell lessons on a "drop-in" basis whereby students can come in whenever they want.

Jobs at English conversation schools are the easiest to get and have the highest teacher turnover. Most of the classes take place in the early evening and on Saturday afternoons. Schedules usually require five working days, but it can be difficult to get a straight Monday through Friday schedule. Your days off might be Sunday and Tuesday.

For teachers with no experience, the standard deviation of pay is not great. While some are lucky to start at ¥4,000 per hour, most receive ¥3,000. No teacher, however, should have to work for less than ¥2,500. Standard teaching hours per week are between 15 to 25. The school will often guarantee a teacher a minimum of 60 hours a month and expect the teacher to work more if there are enough classes. If the school is unable to provide you with your contract's stated number of minimum hours per month, it *should* still pay you for your guaranteed hours.

Materials are usually provided by the school, but the quality will vary greatly. Most English textbooks are quite good, and lesson preparation is straightforward and not time consuming.

Because of the casual attitude among students, staff, and teachers at these schools, experienced teachers coming from the U.S. will probably not be happy with long-term employment here. Furthermore, regardless of your experience and training, it is unlikely that your credentials will add anything to your paycheck. These schools are a good place to get started however; learn how things work in Japan then move on as opportunities arise.

Advantages: Private language schools offer minimal stress, small classes, year-round hiring, consistent income, few if any outside classes (most classes are taught "in house"), and opportunities to interact with other teachers and students.

Disadvantages: Private conversation schools usually have lower pay, evening and Saturday classes, and students that may not be too serious about learning English. These schools are in business to make money, and may not be interested in the quality of its classes.

Junior and senior high schools

These students study English grammar and sentence structure three to six times a week with a Japanese teacher. Foreigners are hired to teach an English conversation class that meets once a week, 25-35 weeks a year. The school year begins in April and ends in early March. Japanese children attend school almost twice as many days as students in America.

English conversation classes in schools require the teacher to be creative and inspirational. The challenge is to incorporate the "boring" material that students are learning in their grammar and structure lessons into memorable activities that reinforce prior learning. Game activities are highly effective in teaching students pronunciation, listening, and speaking skills. For example, "Simon Says" is an excellent way of reviewing the names of body parts. If the teacher chooses, he or she can also introduce new material to the students.

The foreign teacher is responsible for preparing all lessons and materials. Regardless of the age or ability of the students, absolutely no Japanese ability is required to teach these classes. Some schools even forbid their teachers from speaking any Japanese in the classroom.

My favorite lesson is the first day of seventh grade. The students haven't studied any English yet, and now they are alone with me for the first time. They have absolutely no idea about what is going to happen. The surprised look on their faces when I walk in the door is only surpassed by their speechless stares when the class is conducted entirely in English!

Public schools often use a *"team-teaching"* system which combines the skills of a foreigner and a native Japanese teacher. The foreigner plays the part of an Assistant English Teacher (AET). The Japanese teacher will decide which one of you is going to do most of the work. She may have you teach the class while watching from the back of the room, or you might only be used for pronunciation practice. I have been an

AET for several classes and all of them have worked out great. I have heard stories about unfriendly and uncooperative Japanese teachers, but I have yet to meet one. The Tokyo Metropolitan Board of Education starts AETs at ¥6,000 per 45 minute lesson. (See more on team teaching in the teaching section below).

The class schedule in the school systems is very inconsistent; there are very few lessons in July, August, December, and March. In addition to these periods, English classes are frequently canceled for special events during the rest of the year. English conversation classes fall victim to founders' day, sports day, blood test day, as well as all national holidays. Whether or not you are paid your full salary during time-off will be up to your employer, but I always received full pay when my classes were canceled. In any event, there are many extra days off and you can use these days to teach private lessons or do whatever you please.

When hiring for these positions, schools may advertise for experienced teachers with some kind of TEFL certification. As for jobs anywhere, employers will advertise for the ideal candidate knowing that they will probably have to hire individuals not meeting all of the listed attributes. Schools can be selective when they have enough time, but in a pinch they will at least interview almost anyone. If you think you are right for the job and have high levels of enthusiasm, you should try to get an interview regardless of the requirements in any advertisement.

If you have never taught before you should be very careful about accepting a job in the school systems. *You could be in for a very rude awakening.* If you are not properly prepared your classes will be failures, your students will not respect you, and you will suffer a miserable amount of stress. I know, because I have been there! If you are not sure whether you can handle it or not, ask to observe some classes before committing.

Want a real challenge? UTA had three full-time positions for teachers who were *the English teachers* at their junior highs. There were no Japanese nationals teaching English. Instead of reviewing what Japanese teachers had already taught, the UTA teachers met their students every day and taught the language from scratch.

Advantages: More emphasis on education and less on making a profit. Working at public schools includes high pay, time off, trips with students, interesting and challenging lessons, Monday-Friday work, an inside look at the Japanese educational system, and an opportunity to get to know Japanese teachers.

Disadvantages: Public school employment includes significant lesson preparation time, higher stress, long-term commitment of at least the entire school year, large classes (25-50 students), and difficulty in motivating students.

Company classes

For one year, I taught at the Hiroo Metropolitan Hospital in Tokyo. Every other Thursday night I would teach a group of pharmacists after they had finished work. Such a class is called a "company class" because the instructor goes to the students' work place. My class lasted ninety minutes and between four and eight people attended. Lesson material came from a textbook they had used with a former teacher, but they were very flexible and agreed to use whatever I brought to class.

The atmosphere was very casual. As company classes are most often held after work, students are tired and are not interested in drills and repetitive exercises. The schedule was fairly regular, but I had no trouble rearranging lessons when necessary.

My pay for these lessons was ¥10,000 per 90 minute session.

Advantages and disadvantages: The quality of a company class is entirely dependent on the students. While company classes have a potential to be both lucrative and enjoyable, they can also be miserable if the students are being forced to study English by their superiors. Furthermore, the ability level of the students will span the entire spectrum and it is difficult to concurrently teach an executive with expatriate experience alongside a newly employed university graduate who has never traveled abroad. Pay is not bad, but be wary of long commutes! Companies located far from Tokyo make your actual hourly compensation quite low if your commuting time is not paid (usually it isn't).

Vocational schools

For the Japanese students who don't make it into a university, the next choice is usually a vocational school *(senmon gakko)*. These two year programs are offered in just about every field. They are very expensive and anyone who pays the tuition is guaranteed graduation regardless of performance.

Depending upon the vocation being taught, English classes can meet anywhere from one to five times a week. If you are employed directly by the senmon gakko, the wages can be quite high: ¥5,000 per hour and up.

I taught at a senmon gakko called Travel Journal for one year. My students were future travel agents, hotel employees, and tour guides. We had an English conversation class twice a week for ninety minutes. Among the thirty students, motivation was marginal at best. The best thing about my job was that I could do anything I wanted in my classes and did not have to submit lesson plans to a supervisor. As there were three class hours of instruction per week, preparation time was high.

Advantages: High pay, one location, consistent schedule, older students.

Disadvantages: High preparation time, low student motivation.

Dispatch companies

Some companies have no in-house classes. They send teachers out to various locations in the city. For want of a better name, I call such organizations "dispatch" companies.

One of my first jobs was with the Tokyo English Academy (not its real name). TEA has no classrooms. Rather, they hire teachers and send them to teach English conversation classes at companies, vocational schools, and junior and senior high schools. There is a contract between the teacher and TEA and a contract between the company or school and TEA. This is a good deal for the participating company or school because it doesn't have to do any hiring or get involved with sponsorship and visas. TEA guarantees that the school will get a trained (at TEA) teacher ready and armed with lesson plans and materials. Additionally, if a teacher is ill, TEA will send a substitute.

At the schools where I was working, TEA kept about half of the hourly wage, which was about ¥7,000. TEA was paid even if the lesson was canceled, but I was not. This is the reason I changed jobs after one year with TEA. My next job was with a dispatch company that paid my full salary every month.

Advantages: Dispatch companies offer good wages, possible paid time off, training, access to resources and audio-visual equipment, sponsorship, help in finding and paying for an apartment, and possible advancement within the company (management, curriculum development, teacher training).

Disadvantages: Little if any choice over where you will be sent, teaching at many locations throughout the city, no pay for canceled lessons, and long contracts.

Private lessons

These are the jobs that everyone in Japan talks about—getting paid ¥15,000 per hour for speaking English over dinner and drinks. Private lessons aren't always this cushy, but I have never heard anyone complain about lessons they were able to arrange. Private lessons are lucrative, but developing the contacts necessary to get them takes time. After my first year of teaching, I averaged approximately ¥50,000 per month in private lesson income.

While your school may frown upon direct solicitation of students for private lessons, once you let it be known that you are interested in teaching privately you will probably have more work than you want. Use your Japanese friend network to make connections.

When setting your fee, carefully consider your schedule and travel time. Five thousand yen for one hour may sound good at first, but when you consider commuting and the block of time that it will take, it becomes less attractive. Make your private lessons at least two hours per session and at a time that's convenient for you. You will most likely have to go to the student's home. Don't be afraid to charge the amount that you will be happy with for a long time, because Japanese social etiquette states that you can't change your fee once you start. My minimum was ¥15,000 for two hours, but a few of my friends worked for ¥10,000~12,000 for two hours. Incidentally, private language schools charge at least ¥10,000 per hour for "one-on-one" English lessons.

There are really no disadvantages to teaching private lessons. There are no contracts and the lessons are stress free. Pay close attention to the needs and desires of your students; some will want fairly intensive and complete instruction, but most will be interested in "free conversation" sessions free of boring drills.

Head teacher/curriculum developer

All language schools need people who can plan and develop course curriculums. If you have lots of teaching experience and an advanced teaching degree, you may be interested in such a position. Your responsibilities will include course development and selection, teacher training, textbook selection, hiring, and general management duties.

Universities

Universities also employ native English teachers, although they have a strong tendency to hire only those with Masters degrees. University positions are advertised in newspapers, but you really need a personal introduction to have a chance of getting a job. Not surprisingly, pay is high and long-term contracts are standard.

Miscellaneous teaching work

Outside of the standard categories of teaching jobs, there are seasonal and temporary teaching opportunities available. Such positions include teaching intensive summer courses, teaching at a company retreat in a resort area, preparing students for home stay trips, and teaching opportunities with pre-schools and elementary schools. See examples of ads for such positions in unit 4.

● ● ● ● ● ● ● ●

Job Components

Pay is not the only factor that makes jobs different. Too many people jump at the numbers without taking into consideration how their job is going to affect their attitude and quality of life.

Employer's attitude/school atmosphere

Teachers are human beings, not replenishable imported resources. Make sure that your prospective employer shares this philosophy. Most do, but carefully evaluate each employer to determine the type of work environment that each fosters. Do the company's owners or managers seem to care about your well-being? It isn't easy to live in Japan and sometimes you will need some help. Is your company willing to assist you in easing into the Japanese way of life? Some managers act like they are doing you a big favor by letting you teach at their school. When interviewing, try to get a feel for where they stand. If you sense that a company has a bad attitude, leave. Don't let them waste your time.

In fairness, the defensive attitude taken on by many schools towards new teachers stems from bad experience. Some foreigners come to Japan to make quick money through teaching and could not care less about anything beyond their own financial livelihood. They put little or no effort into their classes, don't pay bills (very common), destroy and steal company property, show up late, are uncooperative, and complain about everything Japanese. Remember that as a foreign teacher you are acting as a cultural ambassador for others from your country. While you must be wary of poor places to work, you should also be sensitive of the image that you are portraying to your hosts.

Before signing any contracts, ask to speak with a few of the teachers already employed by the school. Their opinions and experiences should be invaluable in guiding your final decision.

Schedules

From your perspective, schedules are arguably the most important part of a job. Many jobs advertise a total of 15~25 teaching hours per week, but it is absolutely critical that you find out *how* these hours are grouped. As the following example illustrates, a 25 hour job can quickly consume forty total hours of time.

Imagine that you are hired by the Tea Cup Language Academy,* a dispatch company, to teach a full-time schedule of 25 hours per week. TCLA has you teach at a vocational school from 9:00-11:00 a.m., and after lunch from 1:00-2:00 pm. You have the afternoon free, then you take the train to another location to teach a company class at the Doggy-Man Pet Food Corporation* from 6:30-8:30 p.m. Your schedule would most likely vary every day, and the possibility of a Saturday class "…a couple times a month" is scrawled under section 17, paragraph 2.3 of your contract. Your days off would be Sunday and Thursday, and you may qualify for Mondays off after you have attained "seniority."

Split schedules like this one are very common and something to avoid. It may sound like you have lots of free time in the afternoons, but commuting time will discourage you from pursuing other activities. What are you going to do in this afternoon slot? Teachers are never paid for "lag time," and it could be that the vocational school is forty minutes from your employer's building, and your apartment is one hour in the opposite direction. Also, you will have to spend the entire day in working clothes which is a nightmare in Japan's humid weather. In sum, your paid hours will amount to five, but you will feel like you have worked twelve.

actual company names!

Location

Avoid jobs that send teachers all over greater Tokyo. If your job locations are grouped together, then you can find an apartment that will be convenient for work. Many teachers have a great job and a great apartment, but are located 90 minutes apart. The problem is worse if you must change trains or ride at peak hours. After only a few months of this routine, these teachers blame their lack of energy on difficult classes. I strongly suggest that you find temporary accommodations while you conduct your job search, then choose a permanent residence once you have signed a one-year contract.

Training and materials

One of my first teaching jobs was with a group of four children at an English conversation school in Tokyo. I had no experience and was told to "do something fun" for two hours. The school had some English books that were produced in Japan and replete with dialogues modeled on conversations that the Japanese authors *think* Americans have. Needless to say, they were useless. As I was given no training whatsoever, it is further needless to say that the class was a complete disaster. Such an example clearly demonstrates the lack of concern that the school owners had towards its clientele.

At both TEA and UTA, teachers began with a two-week paid intensive training course. In addition, there was a two-hour training session each month where new techniques were discussed and teaching problems addressed. We had access to modern texts and resources, and the management actively encouraged us to develop creative games and other novel teaching ideas. Any quality school should realize that good teachers are one of the keys to happy students. While most teaching skills are best developed with classroom experience, schools should spend at least a week helping new teachers develop basic skills.

Students

- **Class size:** How many students are going to be in each class? Is it a workable number? While forty~fifty is standard for junior and senior high classes, private language school classes should not be larger than ten. While large classes insulate you from constant personal attention, they also require that you have a strong ability to lead and control. Small classes require intensive personal instruction, but will not tax your abilities as a disciplinarian. Assess your character to determine which environment seems most suited to your personality.

- **Ability:** Do you want to teach the basics, or would you prefer to emphasize debate and complex idea development? The absolute worst class is one that has students at each end of the spectrum. In these situations, even a teacher with many years of experience usually cannot win. Ask prospective employers how they classify students into different ability levels. Schools that don't care about their students will group students according to class availability and fiscal constraints. As emphasized above, English is a big business in Japan, and what students actually learn may not be of primary concern to the company.

- **Motivation:** While motivation is difficult to evaluate, teaching can quickly become discouraging if you are easily affected by the attitudes of your students. Do you derive high levels of satisfaction from working with motivated students? Do you care why the students are in your class? Some schools have reputations as being only for "serious students," while others are modeled on the lounge-lizard/coffee-house theory of language acquisition. Ask employers what type of students it attracts.

Restrictions

Any school that restricts its teachers from activities done on the teacher's own time should not be considered. Some schools forbid teachers from teaching private students, traveling, socializing with students, dangerous sports(?), and/or working for any other company. As long as you are doing a competent job, what you do on your time should be your own business.

Housing and living help

Does the company provide any housing? This is more likely for schools outside of Tokyo. Many schools in Tokyo will, however, help you with apartment and phone set-up fees by loaning you money. UTA helped me pay all the front money required to move into my apartment which equaled five times the monthly rent. (This is known as "key money." See unit 5: *Living in Japan* for a complete discussion of apartment hunting.) UTA also helped arrange for telephone service, medical and dental appointments, and miscellaneous tasks that required the assistance of a Japanese speaker.

Sponsorship

Is the company willing to sponsor you and be your guarantor? Companies will usually do this only for full-time teachers, although I know some teachers who received sponsorship for less than fifteen hours per week. Some generous schools will pay for your required trip to Seoul or Taipei to apply for the working visa.

Canceled lessons, schedule changes, and *special hours*

What will the dispatch company you work for do if a client backs out of a deal *after* you have been hired? What about sudden cancellations? At TEA, full-time teachers were required to make up canceled lessons by putting in "special hours." This was time spent doing trivial office work at *half their usual pay-rate!* For example, in one month, if three lesson hours were canceled, the teacher had to work six special hours to get full pay. This was a rather dubious arrangement—especially in light of the fact that TEA was always paid even for canceled lessons!

Completion "bonuses"

Many companies advertise that they "pay bonuses" Rather than extra money, however, "bonus" often means a *completion bonus*. For example, your contract states that you will be paid ¥3,300 per teaching hour, but that you will only receive ¥3,000 for each hour worked each month. The company withholds ¥300 for every hour you work, and then when you complete the contract, you receive the "bonus": ¥300 multiplied by the total number of hours worked. If you leave the company before your contract is completed, the company keeps the money.

Completion bonuses are found mostly in dispatch companies that send teachers to junior and senior high schools. They are also standard with organizations that recruit teachers abroad. For example, both the JET program and GEOS withhold pay for completion bonuses. If the teacher quits, the company looks bad and may lose the contract with the school. Furthermore, it is quite a hardship on the class to change teachers part-way through a term. While a completion bonus should not rule out an otherwise good prospective employer, read and understand the terms of the withheld amount.

Real bonuses

Some benevolent employers do give seasonal bonuses to teachers that work hard. One of my teaching friends and I received bonuses of ¥50,000~75,000 twice during the year. Such bonuses will not be written in as part of your formal contract; they are simply rewards that employers give as deemed appropriate.

Sick pay

Does the school offer any sick pay? While sick pay is not standard, UTA gave up to three days sick pay each year. If it went unused, a bonus of ¥45,000 was given to the teacher. Other schools allow a few days of sick leave which, even if not paid, will not affect salary.

Pay

The absolute minimum for any job should be ¥2,500 per hour. For the inexperienced (but lucky) it can go as high as ¥5,000. If you have a direct contract for a single class at a school or company, you can set your own price. The Tokyo Metropolitan Board of Education starts teachers at ¥6,000 per forty-five minute lesson.

No job is perfect

No job is going to score perfect marks in every category. Don't let a good job go just because you have to compromise a little. The important thing is to focus on the aspects that are most important to you.

●●●●●●●●

Sample Work Schedules

Jon is a friend of mine from college. We both went to Japan at the same time and quickly found teaching work in Tokyo. Our qualifications were the same: no teaching experience, no connections, but an adventuresome spirit and a desire to learn about Asia. Our jobs were very different, and we would have never considered trading places.

Jon: English conversation school teacher

Jon's schedule:

Monday:	11:00-2:30 and 6:45-9:10
Tuesday:	9:00-10:30 and 6:45-9:10
Wednesday:	11:00-2:30 and 6:45-9:10
Thursday:	9:00-10:30 and 6:45-9:10
Friday:	11:00-3:00 and 6:45-8:00

Jon occasionally taught a test preparation class on Saturday for two hours.

The school

Jon taught at a private English conversation school in Shibuya, a major hub station along the Yamanote line. In addition to offering courses in eight languages, the school also had English proficiency test classes, correspondence courses, and a business and secretarial school. All classes were taught in-house, and Jon was able to get to know teachers from many other countries. The school actively promoted interaction between instructors and students outside of class hours by organizing parties and field trips.

The students

Seventy-five percent of the students were from local universities. The remainder consisted of businessmen, housewives, and motivated junior and high school students. Jon found the students to be mature and fairly serious about learning English.

Note that Jon had a split-schedule, something that I tell people to avoid. For Jon, however, it worked well. As his school was located in a major shopping and entertainment district, Jon could plan his schedule quite effectively. He was able to take Japanese lessons at a well-known school located five minutes from his school, and on alternating days he exercised at a private Nautilus club. Both the club and the Japanese school were just a few walking minutes from his job. A split-schedule worked for Jon because he was able to effectively manage his non-teaching hours. Teaching at a central location is conducive to this, and for those considering a split-schedule, I suggest that you see what kind of activities you can schedule in your non-working hours.

Work conditions

Jon taught a variety of in-house courses that each ran ten weeks. Each course centered around a modern textbook, and the instructor was granted full discretion on how to best use it. Teachers could use any supplemental materials they wished. After a few months, Jon was able to cut down significantly on his preparation time. Pressure and stress were minimal.

The best part of his job to me was that he didn't have to wear a suit or a tie! Polo and oxford shirts with khaki pants and nice shoes were all that was required at his school.

Pay

Jon's salary was ¥215,000 per month based on a fifteen hour work week, but he always worked at least twenty hours per week. He was paid ¥3,200 for each hour extra hour worked.

The school was very happy with Jon and gave him three *real* bonuses over the year totaling ¥200,000.

All the teachers were given a "supply fee" of ¥15,000 per month. This was to cover any miscellaneous expenses the teacher might have, such as additional books, video rentals, or field trips.

Teachers enjoyed a ten-day, paid vacation each year in addition to national holidays.

Jon also had the option of correcting papers for correspondence courses. This was paid on a per-page basis and Jon found it quite lucrative.

Other benefits

Jon really enjoyed getting to know the other teachers who came from many different countries. The school's active promotion of student-teacher interaction made the work environment especially enjoyable. A wealthy private student from the school rented a brand new apartment to Jon at a substantial discount, did not require any "key money," and even gave him several used furnishings.

Douglas: Junior high school teacher

Schedule

Monday:	Jumonji Girls Junior High	8:30-11:30
Tuesday:	Kaijo Boys Junior High	9:30-4:00
	*Mitaka High School	7:30-9:00
Wednesday:	Jumonji	9:30-12:30
Thursday:	Kaijo	9:30-4:00
Friday:	Kaijo	9:30-4:00

> *My contract with Mitaka high school was between me and the high school and was not part of my contract at UTA.

As you can see, all of my classes were arranged in blocks and thus I never had to go to more than one location each day. *Kaijo* is a private boys junior high school, and *Jumonji* is a private girls junior high. At these schools, I taught the same level all day. This became somewhat tiresome after the fourth or fifth class, but I preferred this to making new lesson plans. Furthermore, I got maximum mileage out of each lesson plan which I could constantly adjust depending upon the needs of the students.

At Kaijo, the last hour of each day was reserved for a special class which changed throughout the year. This class time was occasionally used to prepare students for overseas trips, but about half of the year there was no class at all. I used this time to prepare for the next day's lessons.

My classes met once a week, 32 weeks a year. There were basically no classes in July, August, December, and March. In the first week of August, I was required to attend summer camp. Kaijo owned facilities in the mountains and at the beach, and at summer camp I taught a few hours of English conversation each day. It was very casual; the teachers wore shorts and I was free to do whatever I wanted to do with my class time. These trips were some of the best experiences I had in Japan. In fact, I would have gone even if it hadn't been required.

Work conditions

With the exception of my Tuesday night class at Mitaka High School, all of my work was through a dispatch company: Universal Teaching Academy. UTA starts each school year off with a one-week training session. The company office had a huge library of TEFL books, videos, copiers, typewriters, and almost anything one needed to teach any kind of class. Once a month, all teachers were required to attend a company meeting where various teaching tactics and issues were discussed. We were paid for the meetings and afterward the company treated us to dinner and drinks. Unlike Jon's school which encouraged teacher-to-teacher and teacher-to-student interaction, these meetings were the only chance I had to meet other teachers from my company. During my work day at the schools, I had almost no interaction with other foreigners.

Location

Both Kaijo and Jumonji were within thirty minutes of my apartment. I had to go to only one location each day, so travel time was minimal. It is standard in Japan that employers pay for all travel costs.

The students

All of my students were between the ages of eleven and sixteen. Because my class was not an elective, student attitudes varied from avoiding all contact with me to inviting me home for a family dinner. I preferred to work with students who were just being exposed to English, and in all of my classes I tried to keep the activity level high.

Pay

My monthly pay from UTA was based on a 24-hour work week and was ¥336,000 per month. I received my full salary whether my classes met or not, and I also received cash bonuses directly from each junior high which amounted to about ¥60,000 a year. Each teacher was allowed three sick days without penalty, and if the sick days went unused, the teacher would be entitled to ¥45,000 at the end of the year (¥15,000 per day).

The company

UTA did every thing it could to keep its teachers happy. The basic philosophy was "a happy teacher equals a happy client." UTA's client orientation paid great dividends as each year schools requested more and more teachers from UTA. Teacher absenteeism and broken contracts were also a rarity.

I was lucky that all of my lessons were in blocks and at the same school. Some teachers at UTA had to teach at five schools, and teach five different levels at the school. These teachers had to spend much more time preparing, but this situation improved with seniority.

While most school policy shuns outside activity between junior high school students and teachers, UTA sponsored three gatherings each year for its teachers and the Japanese teachers from its contracted schools. As is standard with most English language schools, all UTA teachers were required to wear suits.

UNIT 4

GETTING A JOB STAGE 3: SPECIFICS

The Job Search Begins

You have arrived in Japan, stunned but alive and eager. You have all of your luggage and a place to stay. Now you are ready to start looking for that job.

The Monday Japan Times

The biggest list of available jobs is in the Monday issue of *The Japan Times,* perhaps the most well-known English language daily published in Tokyo. It is available at most kiosks and magazine stands, but the Monday edition often sells out before noon. Every foreigner in Japan looking for work will be reading the same paper, so it is critical to get it early and make your phone calls as quickly as possible.

The same edition is distributed all over Japan, but is printed exclusively in Tokyo. Locations far from Tokyo receive the paper one day late.

In this unit are some actual ads from *The Japan Times.* Look through all of them to get accustomed to the way they are written, and then read the following section which explains how to read ads.

How to read an ad

Full time, Part-time?

What does "full-time" mean? To Japanese immigration it can mean anywhere from fifteen to twenty-five hours a week of contracted work. To some employers, however, it can mean forty hours a week. Some job advertisements may look identical: the same monthly salary for full-time work, with the exception being that whereas one teacher is working 25 hours a week, the other is working 40. Which job would you prefer? One of the first questions you should get answered is how many hours of instruction are required each week, and if "additional office hours" are included in the definition of "full-time."

Teaching hours versus working hours

I am always suspicious of ads that state x number of *teaching hours*. To me, this strongly implies there are additional non-teaching hours. This could be time spent preparing lessons, correcting papers, tutoring other teachers, running the English club, etc. The teacher may be scheduled for 25 hours in the classroom and an *additional* 15 hours in the office for a total of forty hours, which is too many. Again, get clarification on what your exact working responsibilities are.

Requirements

"Teacher must have TESL certificate, working visa, and experience." Ads like this scare off many potential applicants, but realize that there is no way that every job will be filled with likable people who already have working visas and experience. Employers always advertise for their ideal candidate knowing that they may never get this person. If the ad sounds interesting, call! In the common situation where the company is behind in hiring, you have a chance of at least an interview even if you don't live up to the expectations of the ad (more about panic hiring in unit 4). If the company is on schedule, it may choose not to interview you now, but follow up one or two weeks later and restate your qualifications.

Of course, if you do have teaching experience and/or training, you qualify for better than average positions. If you are highly qualified and find yourself standing in line with totally inexperienced people, you are in the wrong place! Lots of schools are looking for you, so don't sell yourself short.

Split schedules

Always inquire as to how the working schedule is spread out during the week. As stated above, most jobs with working hours in solid blocks are worth a great deal more than positions that have a combination of morning and evening hours.

"No tourist visas!"

Once again, you can't always judge a job by its ad. While many small companies require employees to have working visas because they can't or don't want to hassle with working visa documentation, many schools include the phrase merely to reduce the number of inquiries. If a company says that they will give visas to people fresh off the boat with no experience, they are avalanched with calls. Always call any ad that interests you! The worst that can happen is that they will say "no thank you." On the other hand, if they need someone badly and like the way you conduct yourself on the phone, they may invite you for an interview. Getting a job in Japan is a matter of personality and being at the right place at the right time.

TEFL? TESL? TESOL? TOEFL?

Some companies seek an ESL teacher, while anothers are looking for EFL teacher. Are they different? No, they are all looking for someone to teach the same thing: English. Generally, **E** always stands for English, **T** for teacher, and **L** for language. Technically, in Japan, English is a *foreign language*; it is not part of the Japanese culture and is not needed for daily activities. If a Japanese person moves to the U.S., English becomes his/her *second language*; they must use it on a daily basis.

Here are some English teaching acronyms that you should be familiar with:

TEFL stands for Teaching English as a Foreign Language.

TESL is Teaching English as a Second Language.

TESOL: Teaching English to Speakers of Other Languages.

TOEFL: **T**est **o**f **E**nglish as a **F**oreign **L**anguage. This is a standardized test that non-native English speakers must take to enter American universities.

AET: **A**ssistant **E**nglish **T**eacher.

JET: **J**apan **E**xchange and **T**eaching.

JALT: **J**apan **A**ssociation of **L**anguage **T**eachers.

Note that some of the following ads are for cities other than Tokyo, but have Tokyo interviews. Any telephone number that begins with the area code 03, or any eight digit number beginning with the number 3 is a Tokyo number

For example: 03-3554-6776 and 3389-5209 are Tokyo numbers.

NATIVE full-time English conversation instructor for a British-Japanese owned school in Tokyo. Over 25 preferred, degree and sense of humour essential. Sponsorship and apartment for the right person. Call Paul after 10 a.m., 3805-3375.

MAJOR Language School seeks NATIVE speakers of English. Well organized curriculum with fixed schedule and location; Kawasaki, Fujisawa, Mizonokuchi, Shimokitazawa, or NishiFunabashi. Paid training and materials provided. For information, please contact Mr. Sato at 03-3780-4445 from 2-6 p.m. ONLY.

ARE you looking for satisfying, challenging work? We are looking for an intelligent, imaginative and playful person, a native speaker of American or Canadian English, age up to 35, to teach English in company classes. The position involves both regular classes and substitute teaching, mornings and evenings. Remuneration: ¥10,000 per hour (net). Please send resume and recent photo to: DLD Language Resources, c/o P. Davis, Central Post Office, Box 960, Tokyo T100.

PART-TIME ENGLISH INSTRUCTOR North American, Dependable and Enthusiastic. Saturdays ¥4,000 per hr. plus Trans./Bonus. TOYOKO LINE. Call (044) 733-8190, 1-6 p.m. Non smokers only, please.

ENGLISH teacher wanted. We're about 2 1/2 hours from Tokyo and we pay ¥240,000 + bonus, Apartment, telephone available. Transportation cost to/from interview provided. Call Rick: 0246-23-7001.

TEACHERS needed for part time evenings. Americans and Canadians only. Competitive remuneration. Sponsorship available. Contact Mr. Okabe, 11:00 a.m.9:00 p.m. 03-3262-2710.

ENGLISH INSTRUCTORS wanted for Conversation School in Shinjuku. Part time and Full time (sponsorship available). American with B.A. Competitive salary and friendly atmosphere. Call 3365-3713.

ENGLISH TEACHERS in Ashikaga, about 70 minutes from Tokyo. FREE JAPANESE LESSON, NICE HOUSING. Call Beavers' English Academy 028472-3265.

ENGLISH INSTRUCTORS hour from Tokyo. using & sponsorship. ¥230,000~¥320,000 month. Kamakura & Fujisawa beach area. Call between 10:00-13:00. 0466-34-5947.

TIRED of entertaining but still interested in teaching? Full-time position open. 6 hours a day, 5 days a week. Very unique system. No regular-type class work. Well-motivated students. Applicants must speak and write good AMERICAN English. Call 3981-0591 between 2 p m. & 6 p.m. T.I.E. Institute.

F U L L-T I M E/P A RT- I TIME Instructors. Highly motivated native English speakers needed by Leading Training Company to instruct business related programs. Enthusiasm, Responsibility and Professionalism key factors. Potential for Advancement in pay and positions. Sponsorship available. Call 35853529.

Prestigious Consulting Firm offers top wages to top-notch, professional GMAT, TOEFL and general business instructors and counselors. Experience and strong qualifications essential. For immediate consideration, send resume or rirekisho, and indicate availability, to President, K.K. Interface, 2F, 4-7-2, Higashi-Gotanda, Shinagawa-ku, Tokyo

NATIVE English speaking teacher for children and adult classes; full or quasi-full time. Must speak some Japanese. Afternoons and evenings. Good program, materials, pay. P.L.S. 3304-5098.

NATIVE English speakers wanted. Solid technical or professional background (finance, banking, accounting, electronics, chemical, civil and mechanical engineering, etc.). School in Shibuya and Shinjuku. Call 54851239 or fax 3400-3812. MBA/APEX.

EXPERIENCED English teachers needed. ¥3,500/ hour. Send resume to Mr. Gill. 6-31-24-401, Jingumae, Shibuya-ku, Tokyo. T150.

FULL-TIME English teacher needed for in house teaching position in central Tokyo. Qualified candidate will be North American native English speaker, who is fluent in one other language. Must have business experience or business degree. Must have at least Bachelor's degree. EXCELLENT REMUNERATION, SPONSORSHIP, COMPLETION BONUS, HOUSING ALLOWANCE, and many other perks. Please call (03) 3234-7841 before 6 p.m.

SEEKING certified elem. K-8 teacher, ESL teaching exp. pref. ¥4,000/hr. plus transportation. M.-F. 3 hrs. in the morning. Send resume to St. Joseph International School, 85, Yamatecho, Naka-ku, Yokohama T231; Fr. Mueller (045) 641-0065.

EXCELLENCE CORPORATION has an opening for bilingual German/English Instructor with experience in Nagano Prefecture. Work in a corporate environment, full-time schedule (5 days per week, 9:00 a.m.-5:30 p.m.). Sponsorship, salary, bonuses and housing package available to qualified applicant. Call (03) 3238-7824 for interview

GENKI NATIVE ENGLISH SPEAKERS needed for evening corporate classes in central Tokyo. Long-term commitment essential. Business experience preferred. Around eight hours teaching a week. Excellent rate of pay. Sponsorship also available. Call (03) 5272-1633.

ATTRACTIVE SAPPORO, Reliable school needs English teachers. Call (011) 221-0279 for Tokyo interview.

TIRED of trains? Native English teacher for schools one hour from Tokyo. Beautiful location, full sponsorship, housing, car, phone, etc. Must have degree. Age over 26. Call Today, 0298-55-7151.

BEAT the high cost in Tokyo. FULL-TIME instructor in Central Japan, near Nagoya. American and Canadian native speakers of English. Furnished dormitory and sponsorship offered. Good working conditions. Call (0532) 53-6101 between 1 p.m. and 6 p.m. Mon. thru Fri. Toyohashi English Center, 1, Ohashi Dori, Toyohashi-shi, Aichi **T440**.

ENGLISH INSTRUCTORS wanted. Salary ¥215,000/month. Housing available. Long-term or short-term. Nagoya (052) 452-3337. WIN SCHOOL.

FULL-TIME INSTRUCTOR IN SHINJUKU. Reliable, personable native English speakers with solid educational backgrounds. 5day/40 net hour week. All work on premises. Sponsorship available. PART-TIME POSITIONS also available. NO TOURIST VISAS. For more information, call (03) 3344-1566, 11:00 a.m.-6:00 p.m. American Plaza, Inc.

FULL-TIME TEACHING JOB: Qualified native English instructor wanted to teach at a well-established high school in Koshigaya City, Saitama Pref. Those living along Tobu Isezaki or Musashino Lines best suited. Good working conditions. Contact 03-3320-0541 ECS.

MATURE TESOL TEACHERS over 30 for intensive Business English Course at prestigious institute near Mt. Fuji. Course lasts 4 weeks, from December 16 to January 17 (with break from December 28 to January 5). Successful applicants will be native English speakers. Business experience needed. Teachers will live-in, teach scheduled classes Monday to Friday, be available for counseling, and enjoy the isolation of mountain living. One day of precourse training will be conducted. Call or send resume to PACC. Tel: 03-33531668, Fax: 03-3353-7230.

NATIVE ENGLISH INSTRUCTOR, required for a full-time position in Iwaki city, Fukushima prefecture. One year contract, starting from January, 1992. Call Mr. Taniguchi, OTC INC. at (03) 35528816 between 9:30 12:00 or 13:00 17:00.

QUALIFIED & EXPERIENCED NATIVE ENGLISH INSTRUCTORS. One week intensive course in Tokyo. Degree & proper visa required. ¥4,000 hr/ plus. Call Pat or Cam (03) 3433-2001 I PEC

AEROBICS Instructor wanted by the Viale Coral Sports Club, near Kanazawabunko station. Experience necessary, proper visa required. Call for details 045-782-1500.

TENNIS COACH urgently required. Work at Kamata or Kawasaki. Please contact 3406-7447 American Tennis School, Aoyama Head Office.

MODELS foreigners/Japanese (professionals and photogenic talents), commercial films/photos, TV programs. Also Japanese managers/interpreters. 3585-5772 (foreigners), 3585-5771 (Japanese). Mark the Best, Roppongi.

INTERNATIONAL MUSIC VIDEO PRODUCER requires native English speaking-assistant. Interest in music and knowledge of business correspondence required. Macintosh experience preferred. NON STOP PRODUCTIONS (03) 3423-0481 (afternoons) John Tessmer.

FOREIGN COUNSELORS FOR OUR SUMMER CAMP. Enthusiastic young English natives who like Japanese children wanted as camp counselors. (TOKYO) From Aug. 5th to 7th or 7th to 9th at West Lake in Yamanashi Pre. (OSAKA) From Aug. 5th to 7th at Towano highland in Hyogo Pref. Meals, transportation, accommodation provided. Call for an interview. (Tokyo) 03-3350-8211 c/o Kawai or, Matsunaga, (Osaka) 06375-4411 c/o Asada. CHEERY ENGLISH INSTITUTE.

GRAPHIC DESIGNER! Come join our rapidly growing publishing firm. We are looking for a Graphic Designer with a minimum of 2-3 year magazine experience for our English language publications. Send resume c/o Anne Bergasse, P&B International K.K., Kamiyama Ambassador 2-C, 1(;3-1, Kamiyama-cho, Shibuya-ku, Tokyo T150. 3460-1195.

FREELANCE WRITERS A hot established Tokyo magazine needs your writing talent. Join our growing team! Call 03-3423-0660. Mon. to Wed. only.

TENNIS Native English instructor. Part-Time, Group Teaching, experience necessary. Proper visa required. 3325-0924 or 3401-2636.

PART-TIME LAYOUT ARTIST Tokyo Weekender, popular English-language weekly, is looking for a part-time computer layout artist. Successful applicant will have experience in Ventura page design and English word processing. No publishing experience necessary but a knowledge of WordPerfect 5.1 an advantage. Working Hours are negotiable, but one 5-day week per month required. Proper working visa required. Please send resume in English to: Richard Keirstead, 2-6, Suido 1chome, Bunkyo-ku, Tokyo T112, or call 3811-7741.

Cold calling

When I am looking for a job in the States, I call on the people I want to work for. I have never even looked in the help wanted section of the newspaper. Sometimes the people I contact are too busy to see me, but occasionally I am able to sell them on what I have to offer. I thought I would be able to use this approach in Japan as well. Apparently, however, this method is not effective nor appreciated in Japan. My boldness was rewarded with many puzzled replies and *not one* invitation to "come in and show my stuff." If you have time to kill, you may try calling English schools to see if they are currently hiring, but don't have great expectations. Listings of English language schools can be found in the English yellow pages. These directories are published by three different companies, but none of them is complete. You will also see advertisements for large English schools in the trains. Write down the phone numbers and give them a call. The only complete list of schools that I have seen is in the Japanese language edition of the yellow pages. When calling, be prepared to talk to people who don't speak English and know nothing about the English conversation classes—speak slowly and in Japanese if possible. Although I didn't find any jobs with this method, one school owner did offer me a great apartment, which I took!

Alternative job sources

- **Other papers:** *The Daily Yomiuri* (English version) also carries a few job ads.

- **Reader boards:** Some of the bulletin boards around major stations and universities have notices for jobs. Kimi Information Center also publishes a thin job listings bulletin. Youth hostels, guest houses, and tourist information centers occasionally have some notices.

- **Word of mouth:** One of the best sources of information anywhere. For networking, investigate a few conversation lounges (a pub where there is a mix of locals and foreigners, and the use of English is promoted) like *Miki House* or *Billy Barew's Beer Bar,* both located in northwest Tokyo. The *Tokyo Journal* monthly magazine also has advertisements for other conversation exchange lounges.

Effective telephone inquiries

Once you determine which jobs you would like to further pursue, the next task is to make the phone call. A few jobs will list only an address, particularly companies outside of Tokyo, but most will have a Tokyo phone number. Find a quiet phone booth (big hotel lobbies are always good) and begin making calls.

Pay phones

It's a good idea to buy a prepaid telephone card the first day you are in Japan. They are available from vending machines located near public phones, and you can choose ¥500 or ¥1,000 yen cards. Phone cards work on any green public telephone. The card slips into a slot and a display shows remaining units. For a local call, one unit—which is equal to ¥10—equals three minutes. If coins are used and time runs out, the line may be disconnected without warning. Furthermore, if a ¥100 coin is inserted, change will not be returned. When purchasing a card, make sure that the price of the card is based on either 50 or 100 calling units, with each unit worth exactly ¥10. Some "collector's cards" cost ¥1,000, but have only 50 calling units. *Remember, a ¥500 card should equal 50 units; a ¥1,000 should equal 100 units.*

Often the person answering the phone isn't responsible for hiring and doesn't know anything about the job. Don't be surprised if they won't answer your questions about the job over the phone. This is frustrating, but standard policy. The person you speak with probably has a standard list of questions they ask everyone: "What's your nationality? What kind of visa do you have? How old are you? What school did you graduate from? Where do you live?..." If you meet the criteria of these initial questions, they will set up an interview.

With regard to the visa question, try to avoid saying *"I only have a TOURIST visa."* Don't lie and say you have a working or cultural visa, just phrase your answer carefully. Good responses are: "I'm planning to get a cultural visa." or "I'm looking for a job that will give me a working visa." It's incredible how well this works. Most of the time the Japanese receptionist you speak with is just waiting to here you say *tourist visa* so that he or she can strike you from further consideration. Getting in the door can be the hardest part. If they really like you, they will probably hire you regardless of your visa status.

Tokyo seems deceptively compact, but realize that interviewing is extremely time consuming. I would recommend only two interviews per day unless you can interview companies in the same area and are absolutely positive that you understand the directions to the school. Attend as many interviews as you can, but also employ discretion and try to narrow your choices down through a few choice questions on the telephone.

Maps and directions

When calling, have a pen and paper ready and especially a good map. The ones provided free at the tourist information centers are excellent. You can also get these maps by writing or calling the Japan National Tourist Organization (address in the appendix). *Tokyo: a Bilingual Atlas,* published by the Japan Times, is an extremely useful map of Tokyo in book form and is available in the U.S. as well as Japan. The complete lack of a grid system and efficient address network give even Japanese postal workers headaches. Finding things for the first time in Tokyo is usually a total nightmare, especially when the directions are given over the phone, so make sure that you understand how to get to the interview. If the directions are confusing, it is not rude to inquire if someone could meet you at the station nearest the school. Or, leave early and call for directions once again after you reach the station nearest the school.

• • • • • • • •

About the Interview

The competition for the best jobs is tough. How are you going to set yourself apart from the other applicants?

The image of the English teacher

The Japanese preoccupation with appearance and form will become well known to you as your time in Japan lengthens, but in the early stages it is critical to realize that your more radical individualistic tendencies will be neither appreciated nor tolerated. English teachers are expected to be clean cut, well dressed and mannered, and highly enthusiastic and interested in teaching. This point cannot be emphasized enough; too many foreigners roll into Japan as a quick stop in their Asian travels and think that they can walk into any teaching job. For your sake, leave the pony tail, three day old beard, tie-dyed shirt, and Latin-American knapsack at home.

Persons of almost all ethnic backgrounds can get teaching work, but it is definitely easier for Caucasians to find jobs fastest as they best fit the model teacher image. I will not contribute to the debate over whether or not the Japanese are inherently racist as some argue, but I will emphasize that your ability to find good teaching work increases the more you fit the ideal image. For example, some schools will not be as interested in Westerners of Asiatic ethnic heritage as such persons do not "look" like Westerners. Some school owners will express concern that the expectations of the students will not be met if an Asian looking—even though a Westerner in dress, habit, and custom—person appears before them to teach. On the other hand, one of my closest teaching friends is half Japanese and this very quality *enhanced* his ability to get a good job quickly as the school owner felt that his mixed heritage would contribute to his ability to interact with and understand the students. Persons of Asian ethnic background—especially Japanese—can expect three different attitudes:

> **1.** Your skin color doesn't make a difference. If you were born and raised in an English speaking country, then you are a native speaker and are just as qualified as anyone else.
>
> **OR**
>
> **2.** The fact that you look Asian means that your English ability is not truly native, and thus compromises you as a "native speaker" in the eyes of the students.
>
> **OR**
>
> **3.** Your Asian/Japanese blood gives you a special ability to understand "the Japanese soul" and thus enhances your ability to become an effective teacher.

The attitude that you are confronted with will vary according to the school, clientele, and interviewer. While these prejudices are unreasonable, it is important that you understand that they exist. More importantly, however, do not let bad interviewing experiences affect *your* attitude. Take your time to find a good employer that wants to hire you based upon your enthusiasm and strong character.

Who does the hiring?

At UTA, three people were involved in the hiring process: Mr. Tanaka, the salesman; Haruko, the manager; and Michael, the head English teacher. (Not their real names.) All three had different ideas about the type of persons that should be hired.

Mr. Tanaka was concerned mostly with image. Candidates with short hair, well-pressed conservative suits with contrasting silk ties, and a good stage demeanor were his first choice. In his opinion, the professional image of the teacher directly affected the company's ability to get contracts from high quality schools.

Haruko wanted people she could trust. Too many foreigners in the past had walked off the job, gone to class late, argued about pay after signing the contract, and generally complained about everything. Her biggest concern was finding reliable teachers that she liked. Her questions probed for well thought out sincere answers, and it was critical for her to personally like the candidate within two minutes of meeting him or her. My experiences with Haruko showed me that qualifications are almost always of a secondary concern; instead, a candidate's ability to engender trust in a short period of time was paramount to getting hired.

Michael, on the other hand, not only wanted people with experience, he also wanted each candidate to be an entertainer—tough criteria and not very realistic. As an experienced teacher, Michael thought it natural that each candidate live for teaching and demonstrate high levels of dedication. For him, applicants were almost never good enough.

On balance, the criteria that Mr. Tanaka, Haruko, and Michael employed are fairly representative of the attitudes you can expect to face in 99% of your interviews. Quickly find out the qualities that your interviewer is seeking and temper your responses according to what you perceive to be the hot issues.

Punctuality

I cannot explain in words the difficulty in finding buildings in Tokyo for the first time. The layout of streets and buildings is chaotic at best and provides an interesting contrast to the otherwise well-ordered Japanese life. Phone directions may sound straightforward and succinct, but one wrong turn and your scrawled notes will lose all meaning. It is also incredibly easy to accidentally ride the express instead of the local train and end up traveling five stops past where you should have gotten off. The best way to avoid such time delays is to expect them and leave early. There is no greater nightmare than to frantically run around an unknown neighborhood with sweat pouring down your face and arrive late to an interview. Instead, leave early, find the school, have a cup of coffee, and then enter the building early and relaxed. Even though your interviewer may sympathize with you if you are late—after all, Tokyo is a huge place—he or she will lose faith in your ability to be on time for teaching assignments. It is quite possible that the school will send teachers to new locations frequently. In this case, the school must believe in your unshakable ability to get to places on time.

Appearance

As highlighted above, appearances count for everything. Japanese judge the quality of a gift by the store from which it was purchased and the beauty of its wrapping. In a similar vein, your initial dress and conduct will form lasting and deep impressions. Always wear a freshly pressed suit, and shine those shoes! By doing this, you will outsell the shockingly high number of applicants that show up in boat shoes, wrinkled khaki pants, a tweed blazer, and a wrinkled shirt that won't button all the way to the top. Make a good investment in clothing and accessories that exude professionalism.

The Japanese do not admire men with long hair and/or facial hair. While a conservative mustache may be acceptable, such accessories place you dangerously close to the rejection pile. For men with ponytails, funky designs etched into sideburns, or the Elvis-look, two words of advice: stay home. For women, almost any hair length or style is acceptable as long as it is neat. However, avoid glintzy accessories and over applications of Christian Dior's Poison. Feminine understatement is the key.

Be flexible

The information in this book will alert you to potentially bad situations, but remain flexible regarding hours, pay, extra help when needed, and attendance at social functions. Know what is most important to you, but demonstrate goodwill by showing a willingness to compromise. As with any new job, it is unlikely that everything will be just the way you think it should be. One clause of my contract required that I substitute for sick teachers if necessary. Thus, sometimes on my day-off I would get a call at 6:00 a.m. to substitute for someone who was ill. Getting a 6:00 a.m. wake-up call was the last thing I wanted on my special day, but UTA did a lot for me, and so I reasoned that it would have been wrong to decline. At UTA, we interviewed many people with a "won't do" attitude. An inability or unwillingness to compromise will devastate your ability to get a great job, so be flexible.

Attitude

While you should stay clear of employers with an "I'm doing you a favor" attitude, realize that companies will also avoid applicants demonstrating similar points of view. Many foreigners think that because they are native speakers and in Japan, they are thus entitled to a job. Exude confidence during the interview, but never come across as being condescending. Most Japanese shun braggarts and disdain blatant displays of over-confidence. Show confidence through humility.

Actively determine what you can gain from employment with the company, but disguise your questions carefully. After all, would you approach an interview in your country with a "What can you do for me?" attitude? Always express what you can contribute to the company, and what you have to offer.

Once you are hired, be nice to the other teachers. The biggest complaint against those with TESL certificates and/or experience is that they are often hostile towards "unqualified" teachers. TESL people accuse those without experience of being in Japan to "exploit the Japanese." But as anyone who has gone to school anywhere can attest, certification and/or experience do not make a good teacher. The most important quality in a Japanese classroom, as anywhere, is the enthusiasm you exhibit, how much effort you put in, and how willing you are to learn. A TESL certificate won't make you a good teacher if you are a bore. If you have good techniques and ideas, share them! The rest of us would like to learn from you. The teachers in a company must work together. How the teachers get along with each other can make the difference between a good and bad job.

Try to get a feel for the relations between teachers, and among the teachers, staff, and management. At UTA, everyone got along well and friendships quickly developed. Often, socializing after Friday night meetings extended well into Saturday.

Show some personality

One of the biggest complaints interviewers have about interviewees is that they aren't at all interesting or enthusiastic. Even those with teaching experience and Japanese language skills often interviewed with a seemingly total lack of interest. Remember, teaching is a dynamic job and requires high levels of interest and energy. It takes some personality to command an interesting class, and it is important for you to tactfully demonstrate that you have this vitality. Always maintain a convincing level of professionalism, but let your excitement for teaching consume your interviewer. It is in this area where you can easily make up for lack of teaching experience.

If you're not getting offers

If after a few weeks of interviews you still don't have a job, don't give up! Getting a good teaching job is, as anywhere, a matter of timing, luck, and finding a company that likes your individual personality. It takes longer for some, but everyone eventually finds a job. The most important thing to remember is to be persistent!

My first day disaster

My very first day in Japan I called an English conversation school out of a directory and was invited in for an interview. Pretty easy, I thought. At the school, I was given an English grammar test and was told to write an essay about my philosophy on teaching English! Grammar not being one of my stronger points, I thought that I was washed up and would never get a job in Japan. I didn't even bother finishing the application. Ironically, this was the first and only test I was ever given as part of the interview process.

Discouraging interviewers

Don't pay attention to interviewers that say "What?! You come here with a tourist visa, a BA in art history, no experience, and you think you can work here?! We are a serious educational institution! We hire only *the best!* English schools are trying to cut back on your type. You should cut your losses and get back home and get a job you are qualified for!" Some schools are insistent on hiring only those applicants that have outstanding experience and qualifications. While you may speak with a few schools that display such hostility, know that they are far and few between. Forget about such encounters and go on to the next interview.

Charismatic types that get offers at every interview

There are some people (I am not one of them) who seem to get job offers from every interview. These individuals have a quality or qualities that the Japanese find irresistible. Unfortunately, I have no idea what these magical qualities may be. If after several interviews you feel that you are one of these people, make sure that you have the job you want before signing a contract.

Panic hiring

When schools are hiring well ahead of schedule, they can afford to be quite discriminatory about who they extend offers to. UTA hired its teachers a month before the beginning of the school year, but last minute changes in contracts, additions, and cancellations often required emergency hiring of two to three new teachers. Thus, every year in March and late August, UTA was forced to find a few new teachers *fast*. In such situations, they often went with the first person that they felt was dependable, honest, and cooperative. (Incidentally, this is how I got my first job teaching in the junior/senior high school system. I was simply in the right place at the right time. Once I was 'in,' things just got better and better).

Matter of footwork

Go to all the interviews you can. Put in your time and it will pay off.

At the Interview

Like any job, this is where all the decisions are made. Your success in generating quality offers comes down to how you present yourself, how well you answer the questions, and your ability to generate a positive feeling in the mind of the interviewer(s).

Walking in the door

Many Japanese employers will make a snap decision about the moment they see you. Assuming you show up on time and you are wearing the proper uniform, here are a few more things to consider.

- **Handshake:** Traditionally, Asians are not handshakers, they bow. I personally feel very awkward about bowing and never do it. The Japanese do not expect foreigners to bow and it is not a sign of disrespect to leave a bow unreturned. A simple nod of the head suffices in most cases. Some Japanese will offer to shake your hand, but I never offer my hand first.

- **Shoes:** As you step inside the door of a company or school, if you notice a pile of shoes and a rack of slippers, you will be expected to take off your shoes and put on a pair of the provided slippers. This will always be the case at junior and senior high schools.

What to bring

- **Passport:** The company will ask to verify your nationality. They will also be checking your visa status. It is often standard procedure that schools will make a copy of every applicant's passport.

- **Resume:** You will need several copies of your resume. Invest time and money to produce a professional resume. As a participant on interview committees for my school, I was shocked at the number of people that produced handwritten resumes. Either use a word processor or have a professional typesetter create a document that you can be proud of.

Writing your resume

When writing your resume, keep it simple and to the point. Write sentences in painfully simple English, and make the presentation easy to follow. Remember, your readers will not be native speakers. Rather than type in grade point averages, quantify your academic standing with phrases such as "graduated in top 15% of class."

Try to include work experience and skills that are relevant to teaching. For example, include the following buzz words from previous jobs or coursework to demonstrate that you have the skills teachers need:

Teachers:	Teachers are:
• Set goals	• Good with people
• Plan	• Creative
• Demonstrate	• Attentive
• Evaluate	• Cooperative
• Instruct	• Flexible
• Entertain	• Motivated
• Lead	• Outgoing

Have your resume actively show that you possess these qualities.

Include other languages that you speak on your resume. Make it a point to mention language skills during your interview as your school may also have courses in other languages. Proficiency in languages further demonstrates your interest in foreign countries, and thus legitimates your desire to teach English.

Although the inclusion of pictures on resumes in America would put most human resource personnel in a discrimination uproar, in Japan it is expected that job applicants submit a standard resume (in Japanese, *rirekisho*) which has a place for a small black and white picture. If you do not have problems with this idea, have several small 2.5" x 2.5" pictures made of you in business attire, and attach these to the top right corner of your resume. Keep in mind that most schools *will* want a picture of you with your application.

Questions you will be asked

Answer all questions as sincerely as possible, and give answers that are thoughtful and imaginative. While you should avoid answers that make a point of your individualism, craft answers that demonstrate your creativity and imagination. Below are typical questions you can expect, and example answers. WARNING: the answers are not written for the purpose of memorization. Never give "cookie cutter" answers to interview questions; respond in a way that suits your background and interests.

Why did you come to Japan?

I've always wanted to live abroad. There are many Japanese people living in Seattle, so I developed a strong interest in the Japanese people and Asia in general. I want to experience the culture first hand and learn the language. I enjoy communicating with people, and so I am excited to share ideas with Japanese people through teaching English.

Most people have a good reason for being in Japan, but others seem to be in Japan due to misfortune and/or mishap. Among some of the "choice" answers I have heard in interviews: "I ran outta money in Nepal. Man, I was barely able to get out of Bangkok and I gotta make some cash. I wanna go to Australia next year." Or, "Well, I heard that you could make some good money FAST by doing the English teaching thing. This is great for me cuz I don't have no experience and couldn't get a job in America." But perhaps the best answer I heard was: "Well, I was only gonna stay in Japan for a month, but I met this girl and we kinda fell in love..." Needless to say, these people were shown the exit rather quickly.

Why do you want to teach English?

I enjoy teaching. Besides learning about Japan, I am interested in sharing my culture with Japanese people. I like being in front of people, and I like to lead discussions.

Don't try to con anyone, just be honest. For one thing, teaching is a great way to meet all kinds of people. It is also a way you can share information about your culture. The insights that you will gain about the Japanese through teaching will be deep, and you will also learn more about who you are as a person.

How long do you plan to stay in Japan?

At least one year, but probably longer. There are many things I want to do in Japan, and I think it will take a long time to do them all. I want to take the time to become a good teacher, and I want to continue my study of the language.

Never say anything less than one year. The longer the better. If you are not sure when you are going to depart, leave it open. For 95% of the schools, applicants who state that they will leave after six months are immediately cut off from further consideration.

What do you know about Japanese students?

I know they are very shy and don't like to make mistakes in front of others. My experiences with my Japanese friends in

America taught me that they are extremely bright, but need positive encouragement to speak English. I think that with patience and a supportive attitude, I can become a good teacher.

Try to mention that you have Japanese friends or know Japanese people. If you don't have any Japanese friends now, make some before you go to Japan! Insights into the Japanese character that you can communicate to your interviewer will show that you have already developed some sensitivity to the needs of the Japanese student. Try to comment on how you can overcome the shyness of Japanese, or on how you can help them learn to pronounce English correctly.

Do you have any teaching experience?

Although I haven't taught English before, I taught piano for three years. My students ranged from beginning children to advanced adults. I also enjoy being the organizer for groups. I gained leadership, planning, and organizing skills as an assistant editor for my school paper, and I think that these skills will help me become a good teacher.

Mention *any* teaching, leadership, planning, and/or organizing skills that you have developed. If you think creatively, many of your work or school related experiences required you to develop the aforementioned skills that all teachers must have.

In your previous English teaching experiences, what materials did you use?

I used the American and British versions of the "Streamline" series. My classes focused on developing functional skills, and I enjoyed creating activities that emphasized speaking and listening.

If you have teaching experience, explain which texts you used and how you used them effectively. As the Japanese have a reasonable grasp of grammar fundamentals, almost all English classes will focus on developing the functional skills of speaking and listening. Emphasize these qualities in your answer.

Can you speak Japanese?

I have studied some on my own, and can get around ok. I'm planning to learn as much as I can while I'm here.

Although knowing the Japanese language is not important for you in your job search, showing that you have or are studying it reveals good will on your part and a sincere interest in the Japanese culture. If you speak Japanese proficiently or even fluently, explain that you would never use Japanese in the class as this would be detrimental to the students' learning of the target language.

What is your approach to teaching English as a foreign language?

It depends on the kind of class and the reason why the students are in the class. What aspects of English does this school focus on? Speaking? Writing? Listening? Travel? Business? Grammar? University or TOEIC exams? My approach is flexible and depends upon the needs of the students.

This question is difficult to answer, and is best answered with a vague response as above. Get clarification on what the school's mission is, and then answer accordingly. Emphasize flexibility, and a desire to cater to the needs of the students.

What do you think of internationalization?

There are people from many different countries living and doing business in Japan. It's very important for Japanese and Western people to learn about one another's culture. I think it's great that more junior high schools are hiring foreign teachers.

Internationalization is the buzz word in Japan, but no one seems to really know what "internationalization" is. At any rate, play along with the game and expound upon the virtues of "smoother cross cultural understanding in our global economy..."

What do you plan to do with your time outside of work?

I plan to study Japanese and do a lot of sightseeing.

If you plan to get some additional work to supplement your teaching income, do not tell your interviewer this. Emphasize that work is first, and that you will make your extracurricular schedule *after* your work responsibilities have been decided. Schools want to know that you will be available, and that your first loyalty is to them. The less said about your private time the better.

Suppose you had a student that kept making the same mistake over and over again. You want to point it out to him, but you don't want to embarrass him in front of the class. How would you handle this?

I would write out the mistake and correction on a note card and then go over it with him after class. At the next couple of meetings, I would follow up to make sure that he understood the point.

You may be asked some situational questions, but I have only run into this once. Use your imagination; this is a good chance to show some creativity.

Questions you should ask

Don't forget, you are also interviewing them. You must decide if these are people you want to work for. It is essential that you understand every aspect of the position. Always ask about anything you are not sure about. An excellent book about the art of being interviewed is *Sweaty Palms* by H. Anthony Medley.

Offers and Contracts

The offer and your answer

If the company is hiring well ahead of schedule, it may give you a day or two to consider the offer. If hiring is for an immediate opening, however, you may be expected to accept or reject immediately. In both cases, read the contract slowly and carefully and ask any questions on areas in which you are unclear.

In one of my earlier negotiations with a school, a few hours proved to be too long of a wait period. Explaining that I wanted a few hours to think over the decision, I spent the day thinking about the offer. While I had gotten almost everything that I had wanted, I thought that it was good sense to "mull it over." Unfortunately, after deciding that I did want the job, I called back only to find that the company had offered the job to someone else. This other person was not more qualified than I, she simply was enthusiastic and ready to work. My concern for making the "right decision" was not appreciated. The company felt that I should have known what I wanted, and that I obviously was not interested in the job. This company wanted people who were excited about working with them. Do not bow down to unreasonable pressure, but carefully think through the terms that are and aren't acceptable to you before you step into negotiations. You take a great risk in telling a potential employer that you want to think things over. My recommendation is to sign the offer, and then think about terms and conditions that night. If you then decide that the position is not what you want, politely and promptly call the school the next day and explain why you do not want the position. The school is not really out anything if you cancel within 24 hours.

Negotiating

Pay at the Universal Teaching Academy was completely non-negotiable. One candidate who was offered a job figured he was highly desired and could hold out for a higher wage. When he found out the next day that UTA would not change its offer and after deciding that it was indeed still a very good job, he said he would gladly accept the original offer. *The Japanese management was highly offended and withdrew the offer!* UTA felt this person was only interested in the money and had no sincere interest in teaching.

Do not accept what you feel is a low-paying job, know what you want and be honest and up-front about it. But do not attempt to add a few hundred yen to your hourly wage by bluffing.

The contract

Work contracts will be legalistic in their language and content, but it is critical that you carefully read the entire document so that you understand the exact nature of your obligations and benefits. Usually a Japanese and an English version will be created. Contracts will clearly outline the following provisions:

- **Pay:** Your remuneration based on an hourly rate, or monthly salary, with a minimum number of hours clearly stated.

- **Schedule:** The hours and times you are expected to work. If your job consists of teaching hours and non-teaching hours, make sure that the contract is clear on the distinction. Specific times may not be mentioned in the contract as hours differ for each teacher, but you should understand the general nature of teaching times—dispatch lessons, split schedules, night courses, Saturday classes, etc.

- **Length:** If you are hired in Japan, your contract will be one year in length. This is because working visas are good for exactly one year. Some companies that hire abroad have two-year contracts—another reason to get a job yourself in Japan.

- **Canceled lessons:** The contract should have some provision for canceled lessons or entire courses. Some companies or junior and senior high schools change their schedules at the very last minute, making it impossible for you to teach the class. How is your company going to make up for the lost hours?

- **Termination:** There should be a way to get out of the contract for both parties should someone become dissatisfied. For you, it will probably require that you give a minimum one-month notice.

- **Holidays and time off:** Make sure that you understand what your school's vacation policy is. Will you get a paid vacation, or just time off? Will you be required to teach for other teachers when they are on vacation?

- **Travel expenses:** It is standard policy that your school will pay for your monthly train pass with which you will commute to work. The company should also pay for all travel expenses incurred if you are dispatched to company or school lessons.

Example contracts

Below are two contracts that I and other teaching friends were parties to. Read them carefully to get a feel for the language and content of what you can expect.

SAMPLE CONTRACT 1

UNIVERSAL TEACHING ACADEMY (hereinafter called "A") and <u>Douglas McNamee</u> (hereinafter called "B") agree to make a contract of employment as follows:

1. A employs B as an English language instructor from April 1, 1990 to March 31, 1991.

2. The basic salary of <u>¥336,000</u> shall be paid to B monthly on a fixed date. The bonus will be paid in accordance with the regulations of the Universal Language Institute on the contract expiration date.

3. B will receive three weeks paid vacation and two weeks paid winter vacation. Before making vacation travel plans, B must check with the manager of A to confirm that B's travel schedule will not conflict with company plans.

4. B must have at least a Bachelor's degree to be employed by A. A teaching certificate and/or teaching experience is also a requirement. B must supply A with copies of degrees and certificates.

5. The contract may be renewed by the consent of both sides. Contract negotiations will take place at least 60 days before the current contract expires.

6. With reference to B's duty, curricula and other matters relative to B's work, B must keep to the regulations of A and follow the advice of the Manager, Coordinator, and Sales Manager.

7. B is required to attend the training program (one week) April 2~6, 1990, before the beginning of classes. Failure to attend the seminar will mean a reduction of <u>¥3,500</u> per training hour.

8. B must attend the monthly in-service meeting. He/she will be paid an extra ¥5,000 for attending each meeting. This amount will be added to B's bonus. However, failure to attend the in-service meeting will mean a reduction of ¥5,000 from B's bonus for each occurrence.

9. B must prepare tests for his/her classes at the end of each semester, or as required by the school. B is also responsible for marking the tests and handing in the grades to the school by the required date.

10. B is required, upon the school's request, to participate in a couple of annual school activities and outings or teachers' meetings.

11. B must attend the following General Meetings of the Universal Teaching Academy:

    August 31, 1990

    December 14, 1990

    January 7, 1991

    March 15, 1991

    Failure to attend any of the General Meetings will mean a reduction of one sick day, or ¥15,000, if B's sick time has been used up.

12. B is expected to take part in a summer course for his/her school. If B is unable to do the summer course for his/her school, for any reason, B's income will be reduced by the amount it will cost to find a replacement for that amount of time.

    > In general, every school has a summer course. If B is not requested to do a summer course at his/her own school, or an alternative course at another company school, teachers will be given the following options: 1.) receive full pay working at the

company office developing teaching materials, or 2.) have an extended summer holiday with a reduction in pay. Prior agreement on this must be reached with the Manager of A.

13. B may be required to occasionally substitute for other teachers at Universal Teaching Academy who may be absent due to illness. It is hoped that B will be cooperative with A in this regard. If B agrees to substitute for another teacher, B will be paid ¥3,500 per substitute teaching hour. If B is scheduled to work in the office and is asked to substitute, he/she must do the substitution instead of the office work. In that case, B will not be paid extra.

14. B will be allowed three sick days per year. Thereafter, if B misses any time of a lesson or is absent from his/her responsibilities, B's bonus will be reduced by ¥3,500 per absent teaching hour. Any unused sick days will be paid to B at the end of his/her contract at the rate of ¥15,000 per day.

15. B is prohibited from entering into any private teaching contract with any school or business under contract to A.

16. A notice of at least 30 days is required in the event that either A or B wishes to cancel this contract.

17. In case that B breaks any provisions in the articles above, A may cancel this contract.

18. A will pay B's travel expenses from B's residence to the school(s). B is responsible for claiming travel expenses at the end of each month.

19. A guarantees the sponsorship of B's visa, as long as B is employed by A on a full-time contract.

20. If A is required by B's school to terminate B's lesson hours due to B's unsatisfactory teaching, or if B refuses to teach any of his/her lesson hours, A will not be re-

sponsible for making up the number of lost lesson hours or B's income.

21. A guarantees a minimum of 24 hours of teaching work per week to B.

SAMPLE CONTRACT 2

This agreement made this 10 day of April, 1989 by and between Aoyama Fun English Speak! Ltd. (hereinafter called "A") and Jasper Q. Sigma (hereinafter called "B") for the purpose of executing A's educational program.

1. B shall work the contract hours set forth by A in this agreement on the basis of the following duties:

    Full-time lesson

    Regular lesson

    Private lesson

    Special Group lesson

    Dispatch (Travel) lesson

    Correction in correspondence course

    Translation

    Proofreading

    Recording

    Etc. as appropriate

2. A shall guarantee sixty (60) monthly working hours to B, and B shall work the fixed hours according to the schedule separately made with A.

3. B's trial period shall be one (1) month, during which A shall be at liberty to dismiss B without any obligations

immediately if and when B is regarded as being unsuitable for a full-time instructor.

4. The vacation covered under this agreement shall be confined to the following:

   1.) Japanese national holidays.

   2.) School holidays shall be as follows: Summer: 15 hours from 8/12~8/19; Winter: 25 hours from 12/23~1/5.

   3.) Other holidays designated by A.

   4.) A shall provide B with 7 days paid vacation. Pay for the vacation shall be paid on 1/4 in the working hours stipulated in **2.** above. It is desirable that B should take the vacation according to the vacation for the annual course he/she is teaching.

5. B shall be responsible for informing A at least 24 hours in advance if and when it is inevitable that B should be late for or absent from B's own class. If and when it is impossible for B to notify A in less than the said time limit due to circumstances beyond B's control, B shall advise A to that effect by telephone or other means available as soon as possible before B's own class starts.

6. Pay shall be paid monthly under the following conditions:

   1.) Basic pay shall be ¥186,000 for 60 hours.

   2.) Overtime shall be at ¥3,100 per hour.

   3.) Dispatch (Travel) lesson pay shall be at ¥500 per hour extra the regular hourly pay.

   4.) Full-time instructor's allowance, which is a special allowance for preparation of meetings, grading, progress report, selection of teaching materials, orientation for new teachers, taking care of annual course students, etc., is at ¥10,000 per month.

5.) Transportation allowance for school attendance shall be paid in the amount of the commutation ticket for one month.

6.) Special activities such as teachers' meetings, workshop, demonstration, annual course ceremony, field trips, etc. shall be paid at half of the regular hourly pay.

7.) Pay shall be paid on the 25th of every month. If the 25th, however, falls on a Sunday or holiday, it shall be done on the 24th of the month of the day before.

8.) Income and residence taxes shall be deducted at provisions of the Japanese tax law.

7. B shall attend an instructors' monthly meeting.

8. In conformity with instructions given by A under this agreement only after the curriculum is completed, B shall make not only a progress report on the educational results but also an advice for studies in the future for each individual student.

9. A shall have the absolute right to terminate this agreement forthwith if and when B comes under any of the following items:

    1.) A false statement made on B's job application.

    2.) Numerous absences or tardiness for some reason other than an emergency.

    3.) Teaching contents in disagreement with instructions given by A.

    4.) Any defamation of A's good name and reputation at home as well as abroad.

10. This agreement shall be valid and remain in force from APRIL 11, 1989 to APRIL 10, 1990 or the date of expiration of employment visa, whichever is applicable, and shall be extended for another maximum period of a year

on the same terms and conditions unless either of the parties hereto gives the other party at least thirty (30) days prior notice to terminate this agreement before the expiration of the original term in accordance with the laws of Japan.

● ● ● ● ● ● ● ●

Your Obligation

Suppose that I am offered a job that turns out to be entirely different from what I was lead to believe. Will I be stuck for one year, unable to move? What exactly are my legal obligations?

Acceptable reasons for leaving

While a few schools may make you believe that their sponsorship of you gives them total control over your destiny for the next year, this is simply not the case. If your employer makes demands upon you that are unreasonable and/or not part of your contractual obligations, you can cancel your contract *and keep* your working visa. For example, it is acceptable to resign in the following cases: (not an exclusive listing by any means)

- The school changes your hours *after* you sign the contract, and the new schedule is unacceptable.
- The terms of your pay are changed from what you agreed upon.
- The company provided an apartment that is unacceptable by *your standards* and the company refuses to do anything about it.

- The work is just too difficult. Some people simply are not suited to teach a class of fifty noisy kids. With all of the stresses of living in a foreign country, do not let your job cause your mental health to suffer.
- Your employer or boss constantly makes sexist or racist remarks.

What to do if you become unhappy

Whenever you have any problems, the best thing to do is tell someone. Do not despair and think that your contract obligates you to misery. Most companies are sensitive to their teacher's well-being, and in most cases they will try to rectify the problem you are facing. My experience has shown me that 90% of the problems encountered are ones that can be quickly and painlessly cured. Becoming accustomed to living in a foreign country and getting used to teaching is difficult and stressful. Before giving up the ship, understand that you will soon become familiar with your new routine and surroundings.

Company vs. teacher

If a company answers your problems by raising threats, do not be intimidated. As the following examples demonstrate, the law will favor the reasonable person.

One friend of mine, Carra, had a problem at a school she was employed by. The school completely changed her schedule of classes without consulting her, and her protestations were answered with threats. Her manager warned that she would never be given a letter of release (see below) if she quit, and that she would have to leave Japan. Carra quit anyway and got a job at another school. One of the school's Japanese staff members accompanied Carra to the Tokyo immigration office and carefully explained the situation. Carra was granted a new visa without a letter of release, and became happily employed.

Another friend, Denny, signed a two-year contract in America. The company supplied his air ticket and an apartment. After one year, he decided that he could do much better if he changed employers. He gave his former company plenty of notice, but was told that he could not quit. He, too, quit anyway and explained to immigration that he had given thirty days notice as his contract required. Soon he was employed at a school that paid him a much fairer wage.

For both of these companies, making threats worked against them. Not only did the schools lose teachers, but Carra and Denny filed complaints with the immigration office, and did not have to get letters of release. The Japanese government does not want to encourage the proliferation of unethical English schools that take advantage of students and teachers.

Why it is important to wait for the right job

Most problems that new teachers face—if not due to culture shock and adjustment—stem from a poor understanding of the English teaching profession in Japan. By carefully reading this book, you will greatly diminish the chances of finding unsatisfactory employment. In reality, there are only a few companies that do not give their teachers a fair shake. On the other hand, I have complete disdain and disregard for foreigners who get working visas only to quit within a month to pursue teaching jobs paying ¥500 more per hour. This is a contemptible practice and reflects poorly on those that are sincerely interested in working for the school where originally contracted.
Immigration officials will try their best to understand problems that separate you and your employer, but they will cast unforgiving eyes upon those who leave companies after only a few weeks to pursue other work.

No contract = No recourse

If you choose to work for a school illegally without sponsorship and a contract, you are certainly free to quit whenever you please. However, you had better make sure that your employer has paid you for all time worked as you are *completely unprotected* in the event of non-payment. Any complaints you lodge against an employer you are working for illegally will get the same response: a free and immediate trip out of the country.

Letter of Release

Anytime you change employers, you must get a *letter of release* from your former employer. This letter states that you complied with the terms of your contract, and that you do not have any obligations to the company. Whenever you change employers—even when your contract expires—you must present this letter to immigration if you want to get your visa extended. Although an example cited above showed that a letter is not always necessary, in the vast majority of cases it is.

● ● ● ● ● ● ● ●

Immigration

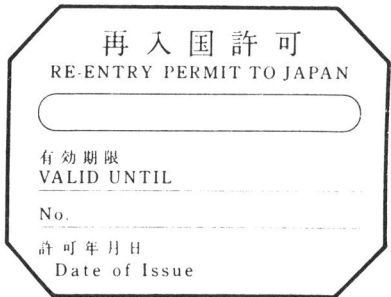

Re-entry permit

If you have a working or cultural visa and want to leave Japan and come back, you must get a re-entry permit. After you pay a fee at the immigration office, your passport will be stamped with a mark (see following pages). If you plan on making only one trip outside of Japan per year, then a *single* re-entry permit is all that you will need. If, however, you anticipate making two or more trips outside of Japan within one year, then you should purchase a *multiple* re-entry permit. At the time of this writing, single permits were ¥4,000 and multiple passes were ¥7,500. If you leave Japan without a permit, your visa will be canceled and your alien registration card will be confiscated—in other words, say good-bye to your livelihood as an English teacher!

Alien registration

Anyone staying in Japan for more than 90 days must report to his/her local ward or city office (the city of Tokyo is divided into 23 wards) and get an alien registration card. After filling out a form and supplying a picture, you will receive the card by mail. Every time you move to a new ward or city, you must report to the city office *(yakusho).* An alien registration card is necessary for doing any official transactions—getting insurance, hospital treatment, and even renting videos—and the law requires that you carry it with you at all times. In the lower right corner you will note that a fingerprint is required. This has been a point of great debate in Japan as even persons of Korean descent were required to be finger-printed until 1992.

When going to immigration, show up early, take plenty of reading material, wear nice clothes, be extremely polite, and *never* argue. As with any governmental organization (lines at United States Post Offices come to mind), inefficiency seems standard and long waits are the rule. For more complex transactions (changing visa status, etc.) it may be helpful to take along a Japanese friend. Also, familiarize yourself with the documents that must be filled out for whatever the purpose of your visit. If I anticipated a trip to immigration, I would go a few days early and get copies of each form that I would need to fill out. Then, when I did make the trip, I would show up as soon as the doors were opened and hand in my carefully completed forms with all supporting documents in good order.

Saving time and effort

Most foreigners do not know that there are *two* immigration offices in Tokyo. The main one is located in Otemachi and there is now a smaller one in Meguro Ward near Meguro station on the Yamanote line. The last time I extended a visa, I went to the new, smaller office and was finished in fifteen minutes versus two hours at the main office!

——— DETAILS OF THE NEW OFFICE ———

1. Opening date   February 1st 1990
2. Name of office MEGURO BRANCH OFFICE, TOKYO IMMIGRATION BUREAU
3. Address   3-6-3 Higashiyama, Meguro-Ku, Tokyo ☎ 5704-1081
4. Services   – Extension of period of stay (except entertainers · 4-1-9
                   – Re-entry permission
                   – Permission to acquire or change status of residence
                   – Consultation for residence procedures
5. Transportation 5 minutes walk from IKEJIRI-OHASHI station
                   (Subway, Hanzomon-Line and Tokyu Shintamagawa-Line)

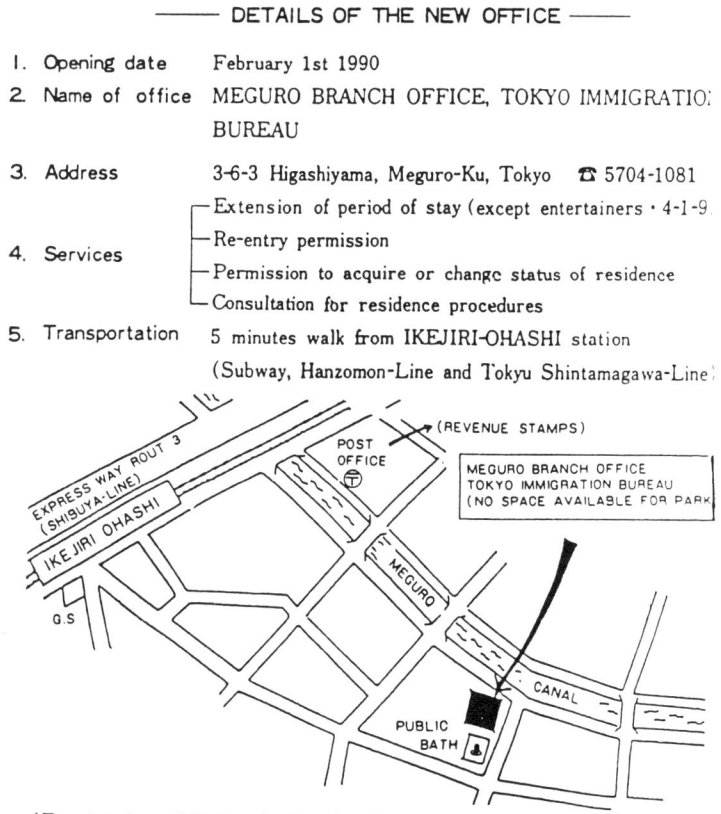

(For details call-Tokyo Immigration Bureau ☎03-213-8111)

```
在留資格変更許可
   CHANGE    PERMIT
在留期限
Until..................................
在留資格Status    在留期間Period

..............................................

許可番号         許可年月日

..............................................
    日本国法務大臣
```

Changing sponsors

You may be wondering how schools can advertise for teachers who already have working visas, when it is impossible to get a working visa without a job. Below is an example which may clear up the confusion:

Suppose you go to Japan in March, and get a job right away teaching for a dispatch company that sends you to a junior high school. It may take them two months to prepare your paperwork for immigration (changing from a tourist to a working visa). It is totally acceptable and expected that you will work during this interim period. When you complete your contract the following March, you will still have three months on your working visa even though your obligation at your employer has ended. If a new company then hires you, it its very easy for them to become your new sponsor. When your contract expires, you can continue to work for the same company, or you can look for better conditions.

Example immigration forms: see appendices

UNIT 5

LIVING IN JAPAN

Living in Japan

Apartment hunting

How do I get an apartment? How much is rent? Housing is naturally a big concern for people when they relocate, but finding a place to stay is rarely a problem for teachers in Asia. As there is a wide variety of temporary accommodations available, I recommend that new teachers concentrate on finding employment first, and then search for more permanent living quarters.

Your first few weeks: temporary housing

Due to the high costs involved with moving into most apartments and the importance of living reasonably close to work, it is logical that your first places to stay be of a temporary nature. There is a directory of low cost housing in the appendix.

If you are lucky enough to know people in Tokyo, by all means try and stay with them your first few nights. Besides providing psychological comfort, your friends and acquaintances can probably give you invaluable job leads and tips on more permanent lodging.

If you are like most people, however, you probably don't have any friends in Asia yet. But don't despair! Before getting on the plane, make reservations at one of the many cheap and clean lodging facilities in greater Tokyo. My personal recommendation is the above-mentioned *Kimi Ryokan,* but travel books such as the *Lonely Planet Guide to Japan* list several possibilities, most at quite reasonable prices. Simply make reservations in advance and confirm before you leave the country and once again when you arrive at Narita airport. To be safe, you may want to make reservations at two facilities in the event that you are bumped off the reservation list.

Hostels and *ryokans* (traditional Japanese inns) are your best choices for your first few nights. Once you have a place to leave your luggage, I recommend that you begin searching for less expensive more long term *temporary* accommodations such as "gaijin houses" (large rental homes that house foreigners on a short-term basis). Gaijin houses come in all shapes and sizes, with conditions ranging from intolerably bad to exceedingly nice. The typical house will hold 10~25 people, with rooms occupied on a single to triple occupancy basis. Bathrooms, toilets, and cooking areas are usually shared. Cost will depend upon the building, but will typically range from ¥30,000~75,000 per month.

When looking at gaijin houses, shop around. While some gaijin houses are notorious for their almost wretched conditions and house primarily illegal day-laborers, the majority are decent, clean, and acceptable. An excellent listing of gaijin houses appears in the English monthly *Tokyo Journal*. The *Tokyo Journal* can be purchased at *Kinokuniya* bookstores in Japan and the United States.

After you are settled: permanent housing

Once you find work, you can start to look for permanent accommodations. Rent depends upon several factors, but proximity to major stations in urban areas is one of the most important. In Tokyo, for example, apartments located near major stations on the Yamanote line are consistently the most expensive. As logic would dictate, choose an area to live in that is close to where you will most often commute, close to any extracurricular activities you are participating in, and near shopping areas. Areas near universities and colleges are advantageous in that they cater to a younger and less affluent crowd. While each individual must decide how long a commute is reasonable, also consider the number of times you will have to change train lines. I personally would rather ride for 10 extra minutes if I can go directly to work using only one train line. In Tokyo, a commuting time of less than thirty minutes each way is considered rather short.

Rental housing is divided into two main types: *apaato,* the Japanese word for "apartment" describing a typically two-story apartment building made of wood; and *mansion,* the Japanese generic word for modern apartments in more expensive concrete buildings. As one can imagine, *mansion* rooms are usually more expensive than *apaato* units. While you can find comfortable accommodations of either type, most Westerners will have to radically revise their expectations of size. An apartment in Tokyo the same size as the standard one bedroom apartment in a major American metropolitan area could easily cost a few thousand dollars a month! A typical layout for a Japanese apartment in Tokyo consists of one "six mat" room, a separate but tiny kitchen area, and a small "unit bath" with toilet. A "six mat" room refers to a room with floor space equaling six *tatami* mats. A tatami mat is approximately 6 feet by 3 feet, and is made of interwoven rice straw. Interestingly, Japanese refer to room size not in terms of square meters, but mat size—this is perhaps easier for them to visualize.

In the majority of cases, apartments in Japan are furnished with absolutely nothing—no refrigerator, no heating or cooling unit, no cooking fixtures, and sometimes not even a closet! Luckily, however, you will not have to go to a department store and spend hundreds of dollars buying basic furnishings. Due to the Japanese penchant for replacing major appliances on an almost yearly basis, there is never a shortage of used but entirely serviceable refrigerators, stoves, rice cookers, televisions, stereos, vacuum cleaners, etc.! Furthermore, as the Japanese do not have Western style "garage sales" to get rid of old stuff, you can pick up these appliances free. I furnished 90% of my entire apartment with items that the Japanese had discarded, as did most all of my teaching friends. Once you find accommodations, let all of your Japanese and foreign friends know what you are looking for. Within weeks, you should have more appliances than you can possibly use. Another excellent source of used items is the "sayonara sales" that foreigners leaving Japan have. Advertisements for such sales appear in the *Tokyo Journal* and are often posted at gaijin houses.

My housing history

After my first three nights in Tokyo at a cheap but clean ryokan, I stayed for one week in "Okubo House"—a gaijin house. My accommodations were sparse, cheap (¥1,500 a night), and crowded! I shared a medium size room with three others. Next, while interviewing for jobs, one school owner offered me a room in a Western-style home which he owned in western Tokyo. The rent was only ¥30,000 per month, and I enjoyed a large private room. While continuing my job search, a friend asked me to share a brand new apartment (foreign-owned) 30 minutes east of Tokyo with one other person. I consented, and so the three of us moved into a two bedroom apartment that featured a full bath and small dining room. Rent was ¥105,000 (¥35,000 each), and we were supplied with new futons, heaters, and a telephone line. Having our own phone line was particularly nice as new lines cost approximately $500.00 U.S. dollars to install. Although the apartment's location in eastern Tokyo was a bit inconvenient, our landlord did not require us to pay the large deposit that most building owners require. After six months, I found employment with a company that was located unreasonably far from this apartment. After searching briefly for a new place to stay, I ran into a teacher I had worked with before who needed to replace a vacating roommate. This apartment was located inside the Yamanote line, and was a fifteen minute walk from the Imperial Palace. Although the building was slated for demolition within a year, the location was perfect. Finally, after living here for one year, my employer offered to *give* me the "key money" necessary to get my own apartment.

Thus, in three years I lived in four different places and never paid any key money from my own pocket.

"Key money"

Key money describes a system wherein rentees pay landowners money up front that is equivalent to five to six months of rent (in other words, multiply the apartment's rent by five or six). Unfortunately, this system is pervasive throughout Asia and is designed to discourage persons from moving often. Of the money that you pay, one-half to two-thirds is simply gift money paid to the landowner, real estate agent, and landlord. Key money is broken down as follows: one month goes towards your first month's rent; one to two months is used for a "deposit" which may or may not be refundable; an additional month's rent goes to the real estate agent who writes up the contract; and the remaining one to two month's rent goes to the landowner as a fee. Although key money is simply a legal form of extortion, most long-term accommodations will require some form of it. Fortunately, many school owners realize that not many foreigners walk around with $4,000 in cash, so you may be able to count on some interest-free loans from your employer. In my own situation, my company paid my key money for me. Many companies will loan their teachers key money then subtract reasonable payments from each salary payment. Shop around for apartments that require little or even no key money. Several of my friends and I never had to pay key money because we looked carefully and talked with many apartment owners. As stated, most places require some key money, but you could save two month's rent by looking carefully.

There are many low cost housing listings each month in the Tokyo Journal (see appendix). Foreign-owned buildings often charge no key money. In addition, they are usually furnished, including a telephone. In return for this service they charge slightly higher than average rent. It is well worth it, especially your first year in Japan.

Real estate agents

Although real estate agents have listings for apartments, most dislike having to deal with foreigners. In fact, an article in the *Japan Times* newspaper suggested that only 10% of the housing in Tokyo is available to non-Japanese residents. Sidestepping the racial issues, Japanese real estate agents point out several pragmatic reasons why they prefer to deal with Japanese: most foreigners don't speak or read Japanese; foreigners are, by and large, transient; most agents speak little or no English; foreigners often want to sublet their apartments; and foreigners throw parties and frequently have overnight guests. Thus, given the long list of potential problems and comparatively few benefits, most apartment owners and agents would prefer to deal with the familiar, docile, and non-confrontational Japanese. If you are tempted to use a real estate agent, by all means go with an older Japanese person and dress professionally. A person from your school or company would be best as this person could act as your guarantor. Some real estate agencies, such as KIMI, specialize in helping foreigners.

Phone service

Getting phone service in Japan is not nearly as easy as it is in most Western nations. Unlike America where phone customers establish service by paying a small hook-up fee and deposit, in Japan customers must purchase residential phone numbers. Thus, when you move, you take the phone *and phone number* with you to your new place (assuming you move within the same dialing prefix). Unfortunately, establishing new service typically costs around ¥72,000. Your best source of help with a phone will be through your employer. As part of your contract negotiation, see if your employer will either provide you with a phone or loan you the money so that you can get one yourself. After getting a phone line, arrange your own long-distance carrier. As in America, phone deregulation has allowed a host of competitors to fight for business. While in the past calls from Japan to foreign countries were prohibitively expensive, today private companies such as ITT and KDD have made rates cheap and competitive with the West.

Upon leaving Japan you can sell your phone line for at least 90% of its cost.

Cash management

The significant appreciation of the yen has made Japan a tourists nightmare, but for foreigners earning a living in yen, life is not so bad! If you temper your temptation to stay out late every weekend night at some of Tokyo's exciting but expensive night spots, you can save up to 50% of your gross income. As Japanese income tax is based upon the previous year's earnings, your first year's income tax will be in the lowest tax bracket. Also, your Japanese earnings are free from U.S. federal income tax (that is, your first $70,000 of earnings is exempt), but you are still required to file as long as you remain an American citizen. Many choose to ignore the filing of taxes while working in Japan only to return to America a few years later and find a big surprise from the IRS. If you have never filed taxes in America, then you can more safely ignore filing from Japan, but if you have filed for several years in America, by all means keep filing even though your earnings are exempt!

Below is a representative example of my monthly cashflows:

Monthly Inflows:

Salary from UTA:	¥336,000
Direct contract with Mitaka High School:	¥40,000
Private lessons; average 6~7 hours:	¥50,000
Total:	**¥426,000**
less taxes:	**21,000**
Net:	**¥405,000**

Monthly Outflows:

Rent:	¥60,000
Food, entertainment, transportation, sundries:	¥90,000
Health insurance:	¥10,000
Ward tax (not applicable first year):	¥15,000
Utilities; electricity, telephone, gas (average):	¥8,000
Total:	**¥183,000**

As you can see, even though the cost of living in Japan is high, I could still save about ¥200,00 per month, or about $1,800. Note that I was earning this salary after being in Japan for 1.5 years.

Banking

Salary payment

Most companies make salary payments to employees once a month, and the money is transferred directly to your bank account. Your employer may be able to deposit funds to any bank where you have an account, but it is more likely that you will have to open an account at the bank at which the company has its own accounts. All taxes are subtracted for you, and there is no individual filing of tax returns at the end of the Japanese fiscal year!

Cash cards

It is easy to do all of your banking without ever visiting a bank teller. Interestingly, while ATM cards and machines are ubiquitous in metropolitan areas, many are open only when the banks they serve are open. Go figure! Bilingual English-Japanese cash machines are becoming more common, but your first trip to an ATM should probably be with a Japanese person or a foreign friend who knows which buttons to push.

Transferring money

There are several different ways to transfer money back to your home country. As expected, speedier methods are the most costly. The most cost effective method I found for cash transfers was to get travelers checks from my bank, and then send them to my bank account in America via registered mail. International money orders purchased at post offices are also inexpensive, but the maximum amount obtainable with one order is $700.00 U.S.

Health care

National health insurance

As a person coming from the only industrialized nation in the world that does not have a national health care plan, the positive attributes of Japan's health insurance system never ceased to amaze me. After about three months in Japan, one of my wisdom teeth began to give me trouble. After compounding the problem with a few of my own home remedies, the pain became unbearable. Within a day I was able to get an emergency appointment with a Japanese dentist who pulled the tooth. The total cost including prescription pain-killers was about $25.00. Over the next three years I had two more wisdom teeth pulled for the same incredibly low price. The quality of the care was excellent, and my dentist spoke fluent English and had been trained in America. Another incident (I tend to be fairly accident prone) resulted in a midnight trip to a hospital emergency room for stitches in my arm. This was also less than $30.00. At these prices, how can you afford *not* to get hurt?

Register for national health care at your local ward office (city hall). During your first year it will cost about ¥1,000 per month. Payments can be made at the post office, bank, or they can be automatically withdrawn from your bank account.

Finding doctors

I recommend that you compile a list of potential doctors *before* you need one. Ask everyone you know for their recommendations, then get their phone numbers and keep them handy. You will find that there seem to be no general practitioners in Japan; every doctor is a specialist. English speaking doctors are abundant, and many in the urban areas have had overseas training. Try to avoid specialized clinics that cater specifically to English speaking foreigners. More often than not, the clientele that these doctors attract are wealthy expatriate business people. It is also likely that they do not participate in the national health care plan.

Learning Japanese

Of course everyone who goes to Japan has hopes of learning the language. Unfortunately, most foreigners come and go without ever obtaining more than a cursory understanding of the language. Learning Japanese is difficult, and is not a language that you can simply "pick up" through osmosis.

Study before going to Japan

If you have time, study Japanese before going to Japan. Even basic knowledge of everyday phrases will make your transition easier and make a good impression on Japanese you meet. Universities or colleges near your home may offer extension or non-credit classes, or you may want to contact your local YMCA or other community organization. Even if you are too late for classes or the expense is too great, at least contact Japanese language professors on campus who can then suggest good texts for self-study, or possibly even arrange language exchange partners. As highlighted above in a previous section, the English as a Second Language department of your nearest university may have information on language exchange with Japanese students.

If textbooks are your only resource, try to get one with an accompanying cassette. Japanese is not known to be a difficult language to pronounce properly, so self-study can yield fairly decent results.

Pronunciation

Bearing the previous paragraph in mind, most foreigners learning Japanese still seem to butcher the language quite remarkably! Unlike the complex tonal patterns of Chinese, the Japanese sound system is extremely simple. The spoken language is syllabic (meaning that there are no hidden vowels) and is remarkably constant in pitch and tempo. As the progress of your students will probably attest, it is much harder for Japanese to hear and reproduce the sounds of English. English is spoken in waves with accents on every other syllable. Treating the Japanese language in the same way, Westerners always seem to place inappropriate accents on Japanese words.

Thus, if you want your Japanese to stand apart from other foreigners' Japanese, listen carefully to tapes and pay close attention to what you're hearing. If you are studying Japanese in a class, insist that your instructor correct your pronunciation.

Get a Japanese roommate

Perhaps one of the best ways to learn Japanese is to get a Japanese roommate. Your best chances of making this kind of arrangement will be to live near a college or university where students are apt to live. Besides inquiring within your circle of contacts, try to place advertisements in the *Daily Yomiuri* newspaper, or in campus publications that students read.

Written Japanese

Three systems

Japanese uses three distinct writing systems, two indigenous, *hiragana* and *katakana,* and one from China, *kanji.* Each writing system has its own purpose, but all are used together and can be read together. Katakana is for writing words that aren't of Japanese origin. The Japanese use katakana to distinguish foreign words and ideas from those that are Japanese. For example, "ice cream," "tennis," "radio," and "McDonald's" are but a few of the words written in katakana. Incidentally, your name will be written in katakana.

Hiragana characters are derived from Chinese kanji characters, and are used mainly for verb and adjective inflection. In both katakana and hiragana, there are 48 characters each representing a specific sound, not meaning.

Kanji characters are complex Chinese ideograms that represent not only sound, but also meaning. The Japanese language's relatively limited pronunciation pattern results in an incredible number of homonyms; consequently, kanji characters immediately differentiate similarly sounding words simply by their shape. Japanese could actually be written by simply using katakana and hiragana, but the Japanese consider Chinese characters to be inherently beautiful and a form of art. Thus, for better or worse, they are an indelible part of the language and culture.

What you should know

Learning katakana and hiragana before you leave will help you greatly. While the task may seem daunting, consider that the average Japanese high school graduate learns thousands of *kanji* before even graduating. Several good books are available to learn these two alphabets, and you will find that it does not take long to master both.

Basics of Kanji

As mentioned, *kanji* characters are Chinese in origin. The characters, which look like small drawings, are called *ideograms* as they stand for both sound plus meaning. For example, long ago in China the sun was drawn as

Eventually it became   Today it is

The Japanese pronounce 日 as *hi*, *ni*, *bi* or *nichi,* depending upon what other characters it is arranged with.

"Tree," was originally written as shown below. Over thousands of years, it evolved to its present form.

We can still see the branches and roots. 木 is pronounced *ki* (key) and means "tree," "wood," or "root."

"Root" can also mean "source," and since books are the source of knowledge, 本 also means "book," or *hon* in Japanese.

If we put source and sun together, the word *Nihon*, or "source of the sun" is formed. Japan is often called the land of the rising sun. The Japanese flag is a variation of this idea.

　　　　　ni　　　　*hon*

Understanding the origins of a particular character makes it much easier to remember. For more advanced students of written Japanese, learning about character history becomes quite fascinating. Many Japanese may not know the particular root meaning of a given character, and you will surely be a hit at parties if you can display some of your *kanji* knowledge!

Strokes

Each *kanji* character is written in a specific stroke order. Let's take a look at the *kanji* for middle: 中 *naka*. It is written in the following stroke order:

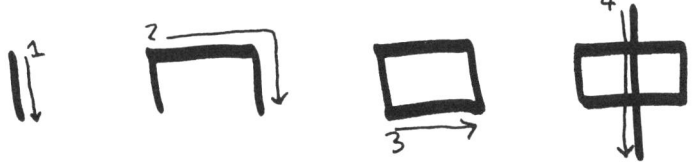

Naka has four strokes, and all Japanese are taught to reproduce characters using the same stroke pattern. One reason stroke-order is important is penmanship. When written slowly, this character could be drawn in any order and probably be read easily. However, when written quickly, without lifting the pen off the paper completely, it looks more like this:

If everyone used a different stroke-order, reading would be even more difficult than it already is!

Another reason you need to know about stroke order is so that you can use a *kanji* dictionary. In most dictionaries, characters are looked up by stroke count and order. *Naka* can be found in the four-strokes section. Kanji dictionaries are relatively easy to use, and I recommend that you buy one as soon as you get to Japan.

Reading Japanese Today by Len Walsh, is a very inexpensive and interesting book about *kanji*. It explains how the characters developed from pictures. If you like drawing or are at all artistically inclined, you'll find learning to write *kanji* to be a challenging but enjoyable endeavor.

Benefits of *kanji* study

- **Map reference:** Being familiar with basic *kanji* will help you every time you look at a map, which will be every time you use a train, which will be every day. Many stations and trains are not equipped with bilingual maps, thus, some basic knowledge will help in locating stations on maps, then finding them again in guide books.

- **Locations:** Learn the *kanji* for the train stations you will use. For the city of Tokyo, the important stations are Shinjuku, Ikebukuro, Tokyo, Ueno, Shinagawa, and Shibuya. Learn how to read the signs for the different subway lines, and the other major train lines. This will help you when you invariably become lost at an unfamiliar station.

- **Filling out forms:** Living in Japan means lots of paperwork and most of it must be done in Japanese. Although there is usually someone around who will help you, many forms merely require you to write your name, address, nationality, age, employer, work address, etc. If you can learn these basics, you'll be able to do most things on your own.

Learning on your own

If you are disciplined and highly motivated to learn, self-study is an economical possibility. There is a wide selection of Japanese study books, but I highly recommend ones that come with cassette tapes. *Japanese for Busy People* is very popular. I have used *An Introduction to Modern Japanese* which is well-written and relatively easy to follow. The five tape set for this book, however, is quite expensive, about ¥15,000. Although I would never condone anything illegal, I have heard of two or three individuals purchasing the tapes and then making copies...

For the solo Japanese student, language exchange is critical. You should be able to easily find a Japanese person anxious to teach you Japanese in exchange for English conversation. Neither of you will get proper lessons, but this is an excellent chance to practice what you have learned and build friendships.

Be stubborn about speaking Japanese. I have one friend who speaks excellent Japanese, and I asked her how she got to be so fluent with such good pronunciation. She replied that she simply refused to speak English. Even when she only knew a little Japanese, she would speak it quickly and with proper pronunciation so that Japanese people would lose confidence in their English, break down, and then resort to Japanese.

You will be obligated to speak English at times, at work for example, and sometimes socially, but not *all the time.* Use your judgment to determine which language to use. If you go into a store and the clerk speaks to you in English and you want to speak Japanese, simply compliment his or her English, and then continue the exchange in Japanese—don't give in.

I was told on too many occasions that "You should speak English, it's easier for you." I would then reply that one of my reasons for coming to Japan was to learn Japanese. If you are in Japan to learn Japanese, resolve to use the language as much as possible. Without strong determination, the temptation to speak only English will become too great. It is entirely possible to live, earn money, and have fun in Japan without ever learning a shred of Japanese.

Choosing a Japanese school

You may wish to spend your free time and money pursuing other things, but if you are serious about learning Japanese, you should enroll in a full-time course as soon as possible after arriving in Japan. School classes will help you study effectively, and the camaraderie gained from meeting others will encourage you to keep it up. An additional benefit of studying Japanese is that through the process of being a student, you will become a better teacher.

Be careful in choosing a school. The flood of third world immigrants to Japan seeking blue collar employment has also encouraged massive growth of bogus "language schools" that are nothing more than visa factories. By registering for Japanese language "classes," immigrants can get a cultural visa which allows them to work up to 20 hours per week. In reality, however, such "students" sleep at "school" and then work 70 hour weeks at tough manual labor jobs. If you become an unfortunate student in such a school, you will notice that you are the only one awake in class! If you shop for a school properly, you should have no trouble finding a reputable school where you will learn. When looking for a school, consider these points.

- **Class size:** The smaller the better, eight should be the maximum, however, many students do drop out, so classes usually become smaller over time.

- **Ethnic diversity:** Where are the other students from? Choose a class that has other Westerners like yourself. Korean and Chinese students already know all the Chinese characters and are familiar with Asian culture. They will learn Japanese *much* faster than you.

- **Advanced classes:** All schools should offer advanced classes. This indicates that students stay with the school for long periods of time.

- **Tests to advance:** Students should have to pass a test to go up to the next level. Performance based advancement indicates students that are serious about learning. A serious school will have tests, and will not advance poor students.
- **Homework:** If you want to learn Japanese, you want homework.
- **Video:** Some schools advertise that they use "video teaching." I suspect that this means that they stick you in front of a television to watch lessons. Avoid such "schools"—you can watch Japanese lessons at home on NHK for free.
- **Teachers:** What kind of experience do they have? Where were they trained? Are they certified? What is the school's teaching philosophy? Unfortunately, many Japanese language teachers feel that the "special" nature of the Japanese language means that it must be taught lecture style—they speak, you listen. Demand interactive classes that focus on functional skill development.
- **Fees:** Do they have an unusually high registration fee? Is tuition reasonable? Shop and compare. Can you get a refund if you aren't satisfied with the school?
- **Cancellations:** Will the course be canceled if everyone drops out but you? If so, will your money be refunded?
- **Observe a class:** All schools will let you go into a classroom and watch a class before deciding to enroll. Demand the right to sit in on a couple of classes, and talk with more than a couple of students to see what they like and dislike.

HIRAGANA

	A	I	U	E	O
	あ	い	う	え	お
K	か	き	く	け	こ
S	さ	し	す	せ	そ
T	た	ち	つ	て	と
N	な	に	ぬ	ね	の
H	は	ひ	ふ	へ	ほ
M	ま	み	む	め	も
Y	や		ゆ		よ
R	ら	り	る	れ	ろ
W	わ		ん*		を

Although written with two separate sets of characters, the characters in the *hiragana* and *katakana* syllabaries are pronounced identically. To use the charts, simply match the vowels in the top row with the consonants in the left column. For example, the characters in the 3rd row, from left to right, are pronounced *ka, ki, ku, ke, ko*. For example, *ka* as in *caught* the ball, *ki* as in *key, ku* as in *cool, ke* as in *kettle,* and *ko* as in *coat.* The other characters in the table are pronounced similarly.

KATAKANA

	A	I	U	E	O
	ア	イ	ウ	エ	オ
K	カ	キ	ク	ケ	コ
S	サ	シ	ス	セ	ソ
T	タ	チ	ツ	テ	ト
N	ナ	ニ	ヌ	ネ	ノ
H	ハ	ヒ	フ	ヘ	ホ
M	マ	ミ	ム	メ	モ
Y	ヤ		ユ		ヨ
R	ラ	リ	ル	レ	ロ
W	ワ		ン		ヲ

*The character in the bottom row, middle position of each chart is added to the end of characters to produce an *n* sound. For example, when added to *ka* the sound becomes *kan (kan* as in *con artist)*. The above pronunciation rules apply in the same way to the *katakana* chart above.

Where to begin your search

There are numerous Japanese school listings in the *Tokyo Journal* (magazine) and in the English language yellow pages (NTT's *City Source,* or try *The Japan Times'* Directory). But perhaps the best resource is word of mouth. If you meet a foreigner who speaks Japanese, ask where he or she studied.

The following language schools in Tokyo all have good reputations. Visit each school on your own, and get a feeling for what the atmosphere is like. Remember to talk to current students!

Nichibei Gaigo Gakuin: (03)-3359-9600

Asahi Cultural Center: (03)-3348-4041

Bunka School: (03)-3379-4027

Naganuma School: (03)-3463-7261

Preparing mentally and culture shock

Dealing with culture shock

Adjustment to a new culture—culture shock—is probably the single item that most foreigners traveling to Japan and Asia prepare the least for. For two week visits, most people can handle the differences that a foreign culture brings. For an extended stay, however, you must give a variety of factors special consideration.

Culture shock can be roughly categorized into the following four stages. *Honeymoon period:* a time of excitement and anticipation. Everything is new, exciting and interesting—the telephones, food, trains, signs, language, beds etc. *Burnout:* comes with the realization that everything that seemed so different and interesting is actually annoying and impossible to deal with. You wonder why the Japanese do this and that when it is more than *obvious* that another way would be *superior.* Some people never make it out of this stage. *Reality time:* a time of adjustment; compromise is made between the things you like and the things you don't. You start to make new friends and establish roots in your new home. *Assimilation*: you feel at home in your new country, and you have learned how things work and can get things done easily. You can make telephone calls in Japanese. You have a list of favorite restaurants and the owners know you by name. Your classes function smoothly and you are putting money in the bank. By the time you get to the fourth stage, you'll probably decide to extend your stay in Japan. It is important to realize that you will invariably experience each of these stages of cultural adjustment. Understanding this process will help you accept difficult situations in stride.

In their book *Asia Through the Back Door,* authors Rick Steves and John Gottberg talk about having the right attitude and how important it is to avoid being an "Ugly American."

They ask, "How do you identify an Ugly American? Easy. He is the one that lacks respect and understanding for strange customs and cultural differences." Steves and Gottberg are worth quoting at length:

> *An Ugly American demands the niceties of American life in Asia— orange juice and eggs (sunny-side up) for breakfast, long wide beds, English menus, punctuality and fast-food efficiency at every stop. The Ugly American sees Asia through ugly eyes. There is no excuse for being an Ugly American. Go as a guest, act like one, and you'll be treated with hospitality and respect. Your trip will be better for it.*

Prepare for culture shock by learning as much as you can about Japanese culture *before going.* There are numerous books, movies, and TV programs on the subject, and there are at least two stories on Japan each week in the *Seattle Times* newspaper. Learn about the issues the nation is facing, and learn to view things from the other side.

Be culturally sensitive. Not everything in Japan is perfect, and you must constantly remind yourself that negative attributes are always balanced by positive attributes. "Key money," for example, is something that drives foreigners crazy. I am sure that it is safe to say that the Japanese people don't like this system either, but they have to live with it their entire lives. The most important thing in Japan is getting along with everyone. In a small country with so many people, this is totally necessary. Don't expect your Japanese friends to jump up and rebel against everything that you dislike like about Japan.

Be open to things that are different and strange. Remember that your stay in Japan is relatively short, and that some day you will return to your own country. For the rest of your life, you will never have to deal with key money, squat toilets, or corn and tuna pizzas. Enjoy it while you can as it is precisely these things that make your experience in Japan special.

I never regretted going to Japan at any time and I never felt homesick for America while I was there. I constantly think about the day I will move back to Japan, and every time I see Japan in the news I feel homesick *for Japan*. Everyone I meet who has lived there wants to go back. You will understand this feeling once you have been to Japan yourself.

Asians look the same ≠ Asians think the same

Compared to America where persons of mixed racial backgrounds and cultural heritages are the rule and not the exception, Asian countries can display and almost perverse "sameness" to the visiting Westerner. Try to resist the temptation to assume that because they look the same, they think the same. While it is arguably true that social structures and educational values emphasize a lack of diversity in both thought and action, it is a cultural blunder to suddenly hate, for example, all Japanese or Chinese people after having one or two bad experiences. Realize that although they may look the same, each person has individual thoughts and feelings, and that most of your experiences will be positive.

Asian people do not desire to be Western

While the ultra-modern cities of Asian nations may portray a lifestyle that seems to copy Western patterns, realize that Asians do think differently from Westerners even though they may have adopted similar business conventions. In Tokyo, the proliferation of "Western" things made it easy for me to forget just how different the Japanese are. In other words, don't let the familiarity of your surroundings convince you that things should operate the way you may expect them to.

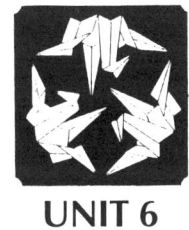

UNIT 6

TEACHING ENGLISH

Teaching English

How, exactly, do I go about teaching English to Japanese people? What differentiates a good lesson from a bad one?

Your role as a teacher

As was mentioned in section one, your central task as an English teacher is to get your students to use English as a *communication tool*. Thus, rather than lecturing to your students about the intricacies of grammar and sentence structure, you will concentrate 90% of your energies on functional, activity-based learning that will allow your students to develop spoken skills. A good grasp of grammar fundamentals is, of course, important as you must be able to answer questions that students will invariably have, but your students will respect and value you the most if you are successful in encouraging them to *speak English*.

Fortunately, you will not have to sit down with pen and paper and each day figure out what to do in class. English language teaching is quite advanced throughout the world, and the number and quality of textbooks is astounding if not overwhelming. Your school will have a curriculum of some sort, and texts that it uses for differing skill levels. Most textbooks have a teacher's guide or supplement which tells about the lesson objective, and will also give helpful hints on teaching the lesson effectively. Thoughtful planning and a thorough familiarity of the lesson objectives will greatly help you to learn the basics of teaching.

Qualities of a good teacher

Attitude

The attributes that you need to be a successful English teacher are the same ones that all good educators need. Perhaps most important is a sincere interest in your students and a desire to share new ideas. Enthusiasm for what you do is central in motivating your students to learn. As you recall lectures and university courses you have attended, you will probably realize that the most memorable ones were those in which you could feel the energy and passion of the lecturer or professor for his or her subject matter. Try your best to transfer a similar level of energy to your students.

Flexibility

A good teacher must also be acutely aware of the needs of his or her students. This means keeping track of error patterns, monitoring progress, adjusting lessons to match the speed of learning, and being responsive to what the student desires in the lesson. It takes time to develop a feel for how a lesson is going, and so you should encourage the input and criticism of students to see what is working and what is not. The dynamics of classes often radically change depending upon the mix of personalities in one class and the students' relationship with the teacher. On more than a few occasions, I have used an identical well-planned lesson that is a huge hit with one class and yet a major flop with another. The ability to read reactions and respond accordingly is important to a teacher's success.

Activity-based learning

The emphasis in this book on activity-based functional learning may seem repetitive, but it is a point worth hammering home. Forcing students to recite dialogues from a text, participate in mindless substitution and completion drills, and/or listen to 10-minute monologues are sure-fire ways to kill interest and enthusiasm. Motivating students is a tall order in any educational environment, but it becomes exponentially greater the more your activities lose their "active" nature. Thinking of functional ways for your students to use language patterns and phrases demands some work and creativity, but it is far better than *having* to teach grammar and composition! All language learning requires book study and countless hours of mastering grammar and sentence structure fundamentals, but remember that your job as a conversation teacher is to give students a break from rote learning through encouraging activity-based learning. Specific details and examples will follow below.

Lesson planning

For a lesson to go over well with your students, it must be well conceived and developed. Lesson planning is important for all teachers of any experience level, but it is especially critical for your early stages. Later, after you have used a textbook for several classes and learn how to gauge students' reactions to your lessons, you will be able to greatly reduce lesson preparation time and make adjustments during a lesson.

As mentioned above, it is not necessary for you to sit down and develop a lesson from scratch with nothing but a piece of blank paper. Most modern English texts are quite good, and a careful reading of the teacher's supplement will greatly enhance your presentation readiness. The importance of creativity comes in when you read what the lesson objective is, and then think about the needs of your students. I usually asked myself, "What kind of an activity can I think of that is fun, and will reinforce the lesson point?" The challenge in planning a good lesson is to develop ideas for activities that combine lesson objectives with activities that are enjoyable for you and the students.

Good and bad lessons

A bad lesson

Bad lessons begin with a total lack of preparation by the teacher. In a typical scenario, the teacher arrives to class, begins an exercise without any kind of introduction, fumbles with a tape that has not been fast-forwarded to the right section, and leads the students in activities they don't understand. The teacher is obviously flustered, and the reaction of the students only exacerbates the situation. In a bad lesson, the teacher lectures to the students for minutes on end, and does not give them adequate opportunities to speak themselves. Activities, if there are any, have no purpose to the lesson objective and are not well understood by the participants.

A good lesson

Good lessons begin with preparation. The teacher has read through the lesson several times, understands the point of the lesson, and has developed activities that are easy to explain and directly relate to the lesson objective. The teacher has anticipated problem areas, and has come up with ways to handle such difficulties. Tapes, if implemented, are tested for comprehension and wound to the correct starting point. Teacher talk time is minimal, and the teacher presents the lesson points in a way that is easy to follow. Pair and small group activities are devised so that student talk time is maximized.

An example lesson

Although the task of teaching requires high levels of energy and creativity, it should be clear that most teaching blunders are avoidable through preparation. Well thought out lessons will give you confidence, and the positive reaction you get from students will be quite rewarding. Developing fun and educational lessons is not hard. Although texts give suggestions on how to present material, there is plenty of room for creativity. Moreover, many of the suggestions that texts give are rather bland and boring. But even material that seems lifeless and boring on its face can be made into successful lessons. As an example, please follow along and look at the next page.

Finding the Best Jobs 145

Jessica: My big brother's really great. He's big and strong.
Angela: Well my big brother can do anything.
Jessica: Oh yeah? What can he do?
Angela: He's a really good cook. He can cook anything.
Jessica: What dishes can he cook?
Angela: He can cook hamburgers, spaghetti, steak, and eggs.

Jessica: Well my brother is a great musician. He can play lots of instruments.
Angela: Which ones?
Jessica: He can play the piano, guitar, drums, and the violin. Can your brother play the violin?
Angela: No he can't, but he can speak Chinese, Spanish, and Italian.
Jessica: My sister can speak Chinese. She's smart too. She can...

Above is a model of a typical page out of an English conversation textbook. How can a lesson be planned from this? Can interesting activities be developed? What are some creative ways in which the material might be changed? Read on for an example lesson!

The example lesson printed below is quite typical of what you may expect to see from your textbooks. At many schools, you will be given a textbook and simply told to begin with lesson 15. That's it! How would you develop a lesson around the information on the page below? Here are some ideas and approaches that I have used:

STEP 1: Identify the target structure

Always begin by identifying what the central idea of the lesson is. In the example, students learn about the verb *can*.

STEP 2: Use the dialogue creatively

An inexperienced teacher would most likely have students open to the lesson page and then simply play the dialogue tape while students read quietly. Under these circumstances, many students will neither listen nor read along. To motivate them to listen, tell students to close their texts while listening. After playing the tape through twice, hand out a revised copy of the dialogue that has portions of the conversation whited out. Play the tape through several times and then have the students fill in the blanks. Another option is to retype the dialogue with mistakes and then have students identify the incorrect words. This listening technique also works well with popular songs. I have often used a capella songs such as Suzanne Vega's *Tom's Diner* and Billy Joel's *For the Longest Time* for listening practice. Often, students will sing along after they have filled in missing words.

Next, students can practice the dialogue in pairs as you walk around the room to monitor them. For my junior and senior high school classes, I often required the students to memorize the dialogues. In class, I would ask several pairs of students to come to the front of the class and recite the dialogue by memory. This technique was quite effective in getting students to study hard!

STEP 3: Activities that stress ACTION

A simple activity that I use with this lesson is to make all students stand next to their desks and make a sentence about themselves or someone they know. Before the student can sit down, she must say, for example, "I can ride a bicycle." If the sentence is correct and hasn't been used yet, the student can sit down.

Next, give the students a sheet with the following incomplete sentences on it:

Find someone who can:

play baseball_____

play the piano_____

speak English_____

drive a car_____

swim_____

bake a cake_____

Students take the sheet and ask their classmates "can" questions and then fill in names only when they find someone who can do the stated action. I usually list approximately 20 statements with the restriction that a student's name not appear more than three times. In order for this activity to be effective, you must demonstrate it to the students and insist that no Japanese be spoken. I also include a question phrase that only I can do—in the above case, drive a car. This ensures that all students will participate as each one must ask me if I can drive a car.

It is essential that you carefully explain and demonstrate to students how a given activity should work. Just as importantly, demonstrate how an activity should *not* be done. For example, in the activity above, these are some of the problems you will encounter if no instruction is given: 1.) students will speak to each other in Japanese; 2.) students will copy names from other students' forms; and 3.) students will not ask questions to individuals; instead they will merely ask a group of students "Can you...?" Students often speed through activities as if the first one to finish wins a prize. I always emphasize that the point of the activity is doing it well—not quickly.

Through a little creativity, it is clear that you can take a "standard" lesson and make it interesting and educational for the students. With time, your creativity will grow and you will quickly learn how to develop activities that are effective.

Teaching adults, students, and children

Adults

Most of the adults you encounter in your classes will be, more likely than not, business people (especially men) forced or "encouraged" to take English lessons by their superiors. Perhaps the key difficulty you will face as their teacher is motivation and energy level. After all, after putting in an eight to ten hour day, how motivated would *you* be to study English for an additional hour? And, what kind of feelings would you have toward any foreign teacher that forced you to participate in tiring and stressful activities? When teaching any person who has already had a full day of work and the assorted stresses that accompany it, it is critical that the English lesson be relaxing and low-key. This means that you should not push your business students to work on complex activities that require high energy and concentration levels. Incorporate several listening activities as these focus on reactive-based learning. Also, inject steady doses of humor into the lesson to make it an enjoyable experience. Company classes are a great example of how teaching in its purest form must give way to the wants of the student-client. Keep in mind that company executives often require that subordinates take English not to become fluent speakers, but to merely get used to interacting with a native English speaker. If you can humor your students, keep them awake, and apprise them now and then of useful personal and business customs of English speakers, you will have completely succeeded in your task.

Junior and senior high school students

Whereas students at private language schools voluntarily choose to learn English, students at junior and senior high schools are forced to study English. Consequently, you can anticipate having to act now and then as a disciplinarian to maintain order and command respect. Japanese school children are on the whole quite well behaved, but it is important for them to know that you, although a foreigner, are in charge and that you are not afraid to demand order.

At many schools, "team teaching" (wherein a native Japanese English teacher is paired with a native English speaking Westerner) has become popular. Team teaching is supposed to unite the strengths of a native speaker with that of a Japanese teacher, but in reality it is quite difficult to accomplish smoothly. The biggest problem is that it is not usually clear who will be responsible for lesson planning. An inability to communicate ideas causes additional difficulties, and thus coordination of activities with lessons is hampered. Students seem to treat the Westerner as an external appendage of the Japanese teacher, and often respond only to the Japanese teacher who is only too willing to translate any instructions you may give into Japanese. The best team teaching experiences are those in which the Japanese teacher discusses the lesson objective with you, and then lets you teach it with activities that you deem appropriate and beneficial.

The logistics of a classroom containing 45~55 students mandate that activities be constructed quite differently than those for classes of 5~10 students. Student attention spans are short, so you must emphasize pair activities that take little time. An effective technique for energetic students is called "TPR" or *total physical response.* TPR activities include those that require body movement in response to verbal commands. Games such as "Simon Says" are quite effective in concentrating energy for short periods of time. In large classes, attention that you give to individual students must be cut to a minimum. If a student's mistake cannot be corrected quickly, note the mistake on a card and discuss the matter with the student after class.

Your role in the class will be to attempt to develop conversation and listening comprehension skills, but remember that such skills are not tested in the rigorous university entrance examinations. Thus, it will be difficult for students to take your class lessons as seriously as you might hope. Just as with the companies that require their employees to study English, many school boards are interested in having students gain exposure to Westerners—not learn real conversation skills.

You will be expected to formally evaluate students 3 or 4 times a year. You may or may not be responsible for developing tests and evaluation procedures, but you will most likely at least have a strong say in the criteria for evaluation. In my classes, I instituted an evaluation procedure that worked quite well. Rather than base my evaluations strictly on test scores, I gave heavy weight to effort. On a one page seating chart, I made comments throughout the term for each student and reviewed these comments with the student and other teachers. My simple evaluation form consisted of the following code:

t = talking in class

E = good effort, **e** = poor effort

Q = good scores on quizzes, **q** = low scores on quizzes

H = homework in on time, **h** = homework incomplete/not on time

At the end of the term, I ranked students on a 1~6 scale, 1 representing outstanding effort and achievement, and 6 representing an almost total lack of effort.

Warning: after taking my seminar, many people reflect on my positive experiences in the Japanese educational system and thus decide that they too want to teach in junior and senior high schools. Part of the reason why my experience was so great was because I was teaching at highly ranked private schools. As most of my students would most likely go on to prestigious colleges and universities, teaching them was a pleasure. At lower level schools, however, many English teachers have a difficult time establishing any kind of order and complain of poorly motivated students. Prepare yourself for the possibility of having to teach a wide variety of students if you choose to teach within the educational system.

Children

More and more children are beginning to study English—some as early as 4 or 5 years old. Teaching children, although exciting, is one of the biggest challenges of any teacher. First of all, it is hard to look at the world through the eyes of a child. Whereas it is relatively easy to meet the intellectual demands of an adult or even adolescent learner, understanding how children think is an education within itself.

Unless you have lots of experience teaching and/or just love children, I would advise that you think carefully about teaching children under 9 years old as it will become a nightmare just to control them—especially in a foreign language! You will quickly discover that your verbal admonishments are falling on deaf ears. A friend of mine taught a group of 10-year-old girls and did, however, have a positive experience. They were well-behaved to begin with, he could speak Japanese, and they had already mastered the alphabet under a different teacher. By using coloring books and a wide variety of TPR activities, my friend was able to create lessons that were fun and stimulating. His main advice: activities must not last longer than 5 minutes! Attention spans of children are incredibly short, and they become restless quickly. Also, have mini-breaks in the lesson every 20 minutes, and never teach longer than 50 minutes. The biggest benefit of teaching children is your own cultural education. It is an absolutely fascinating way to view first-hand how children in different societies assimilate information.

Private lessons

Teaching private lessons is perhaps the most monetarily rewarding form of instruction. Hourly pay is quite high, with ¥5,000 per hour a fairly standard minimum. In fact, many schools charge customers up to ¥10,000 or even ¥15,000 for hourly one-to-one instruction. Your school may have provisions for private instruction, but it is most likely that you will cultivate a private student base on your own.

As in any kind of individual-based instruction, private lessons focus on the learning desires of the student. Because the nature of the instruction is so personal, it is important that you quickly establish what the learning priorities of the student are. Here are some questions you and your private student should consider: How serious is the student? Does the student expect hard-core drilling, or simple conversation development? Will a textbook be used? What does the student want from the lessons?

While the reasons for taking private English lessons widely vary, almost all private students desire long periods of unstructured conversation—often called "free conversation." Teaching becomes less formal as the teacher attempts to help the student develop natural and more highly developed levels of discussion. If the student's level of comprehension is high, then you may be able to use articles from newsmagazines and newspapers for reading practice, vocabulary build-up, and as a conversation topic. Find out what the student's interests are, and then choose articles accordingly.

I found that ninety-minute to two-hour private lessons worked the best. Unless the location for a lesson is a school classroom, one hour just does not seem to provide enough time for a good lesson with time for review at the end. If you are meeting the student at his or her home, arrange that your train fare be included in the lesson fee.

Teaching aids and how to use them

Besides the standard textbook that you will most likely be teaching from, there are several other teaching aids that you can use for variety. Below is a brief discussion of some of the more popular items, and ways in which they can be used.

Audio tapes:

Tapes are a great way to give students listening practice. Tapes require students to listen critically and become accustomed to the rhythm and accent of English. Encourage students to practice the dialogues out loud while mimicking the character and pitch of the words.

Games:

It is quite easy to modify games such as "Pictionary" for use in class. In pairs, you can have students come to the front of the class and then show them a card with a noun, verb, or adjective written on it. The students must then draw pictures describing the word on the blackboard. Another game that is popular is to give a student a card with the name of a famous celebrity on it and then have the student give the other students "clues." For example, a student that has been given a card with the name "Madonna" on it can say to the class, "I am very sexy and I sing pop songs." The main point is that games encourage learning through their fun nature.

My first day activity:

On the first day of a new class, I hand out a sheet containing questions about me. I then give the students a short speech about myself and have the students circle or fill in the appropriate answers on the sheet. The length and complexity of your speech and the questions can be tempered to the students' ability. Students enjoy this activity as they will be quite curious to know more about you, and it is a great way for you to introduce yourself to them.

Problems all teachers face

Do not let your students depend upon their native language in class. At times it is probably inevitable that a few words of Japanese or Korean be spoken in class, but quickly enforce the idea that you will not tolerate "interpreters." Students of lower ability will often turn hopeful eyes to their classmates when they don't understand what you ask or say. In these cases, keep asking the student using simpler phrases and/or hand motions and do not allow others to fill in missing ideas.

Insist that your students strive for proper pronunciation. Japanese is an interesting language in that many foreign loan words have been incorporated into the language with the caveat that the foreign *pronunciation* is *not* borrowed! Thus, many of my students would speak to me in "Japanglish" and pronounce words such as "tennis" as *tenisu* or "computer" as *computaa*. Although your ear will quickly get used to this method of pronunciation, force them to practice good speech.

It is important to realize that no matter how hard you try to be a good teacher, you will not be able to satisfy all of your students. Don't worry about being everything to everyone. While some of your lessons will go incredibly well, others will probably flop. This is a natural part of teaching, and you will learn something from both your good and bad lessons. The important thing is to try new things, have fun, and learn from your successes as well as your mistakes.

UNIT 7

BEYOND TEACHING

Beyond Teaching

How long will I teach in Asia? What possibilities for other work are there? Where will teaching take me?

Form a long range plan

There is no doubt that teaching English in any Asian country will open your eyes to the world and allow you to have myriad experiences unavailable in your own country. I am sure that your experiences and memories will be indelibly etched in your mind and that your plans for the future may be significantly altered after your Asian experiences. However, throughout your stay always think about what you will do after you finish teaching. While most that go to Asia view teaching English as a temporary cultural experience, the good money and satisfying lifestyle often make it all too easy to forget about forging plans for the future. Moreover, your salary will no doubt allow you a standard of living greater than what you could have back home—especially when you consider the pay for the hours worked.

Keep in mind that future employers may admire your cultural inquisitiveness and spirit of adventure in going to Asia, but they will not reward this experience with great "international" job offers. Unless you plan on pursuing a graduate degree in education, teaching will not be considered extremely relevant work experience. The shock for many ex-teachers coming back to America from $25.00~50.00 an hour jobs is rather severe. Stay in Asia at least a year, but heavily weigh the benefit and costs of additional time. If you are learning the language or pursuing other career interests additional time is certainly warranted. Think about what you want to do, and then make a plan.

Finally, working in Asia is like going to college: if you do nothing to prepare for graduation, then you will find yourself on the street with no skills, connections, marketable experience, or prospects.

Non-teaching jobs

For those interested in pursuing non-teaching jobs, the opportunities are significant depending upon the skills that you have and, most importantly, your perseverance. There are many foreigners working in Japan in capacities including all areas of business, photographers, translators, writers, models, etc. As connections are critically important in Japan—especially for service related jobs—teaching will allow you to earn a living while using your free time to make contacts with others in your line of work. Photography is my area of interest, and my networking activities with other photographers in Tokyo yielded excellent results. In fact, by my third year, I was earning more money as a photographer than as a teacher. An excellent way to meet people interested in doing things you are interested in is to join your country's chamber of commerce in Tokyo, or at least go to its meetings and events.

It is important that you bring with you all the tools of your trade, and have several copies of your work in a professional portfolio. If you are truly interested in pursuing, for example, magazine article writing, then bring your word processor, printer, and several high quality copies of some of your best work.

Although you shouldn't count on full-time work outside the English industry when you first arrive, it is still very possible to pursue the work that interests you. In my case, I was able to gradually reduce my extracurricular teaching hours (only a few per week) so that I still had plenty of time for my increasing photography obligations. In a similar vein, you can use your teaching job as your principle source of income, and then devote the rest of your schedule to developing your area of interest. This way, you won't have to worry about changing your visa status or trying to get a working visa for your true area of interest.

In conclusion, no matter what your professional interests are, you can develop this talent in Japan if you work hard to make connections and are patient. A good resource to consult for further information is Terra Brockman's *The Job Hunter's Guide to Japan*. In this book, Brockman gives concise and straightforward advice for those interested in developing work prospects outside of teaching.

Working for Japanese Companies

Work at a Japanese company can give you excellent experience that employers in your home country will value—especially if you can combine this experience with technical skills and a strong grasp of the language and culture. Keep in mind, however, that your ability to contribute to a Japanese firm will most likely be constrained by your language skills. This point is worth pondering: if your knowledge of spoken and written Japanese is not near fluent, you will be severely limited in what you can do. Many foreign staff members of Japanese firm international departments complain of being allowed only to write letters in English and/or other menial tasks, but they do not seem to see the close connection between ability to communicate completely and greater levels of responsibility. For highly skilled computer science software engineers or computer-based derivative option modeling rocket scientists that work for investment banks, you can leave your Japanese skills at home and still be in demand. But for most other foreigners, *study the language diligently if you hope to get anywhere.*

At any rate, an excellent book on this subject is Robert M. March's *Working for a Japanese Company: Insights into the Multicultural Workplace*. This book should be *required reading* for anyone considering working in Japan or another country for a Japanese corporation.

AFTERWORD

This book was designed to help those interested in Asia to get the best jobs possible. Although there are no guarantees for anyone, if you go abroad properly prepared and with a sincere interest in that country's people and culture, your chances for success are great.

Although this book contains details of my life in Japan, expect your experience abroad to be unique. Each of us will be affected differently by what we find in Asia. Take advantage of this opportunity to get an international education. Examine and learn from the cultural differences that challenge you.

Although the job market will fluctuate with the economy, there will always be a demand for native English teachers in Asia.

We would like to hear about your experience. Please send your tips, comments and suggestions.

Gambate!

Appendices

Recommended reading

A Guide to Teaching English in Japan by Charles B. Wordell. An in-depth look at English in Japan.

Asia Through the Back Door by Rick Steves and John Gottenberg. How to travel on a budget and get the most out of your time abroad.

Culture Shock! Japan, Thailand, etc. various authors. Very helpful in understanding contemporary clashes between eastern and western cultures.

How to Use the Post Office An English guide published by the Japanese post office and available for free at any post office in Japan.

Japan-Think, Ameri-Think by Robert J. Collins. "An irreverent guide to understanding the cultural differences between us."

Jobs in Japan by John Wharton. This has a good overview of life as an English teacher in Japan.

Lonely planet guide to Japan and *Gateway to Japan* guide books. Use these for finding accommodations and other travel-essentials.

Read Japanese Today by Len Walsh. An explanation of the kanji writing system. This book will help you understand and remember the characters.

Sweaty Palms by Anthony Medley "The neglected art of being interviewed." Understand the interview process and what employers are looking for. Learn how to take control of an interview. This is definitely a book I should have read before I moved to Japan.

Teaching English Abroad. by Susan Griffith. A country by country guide to finding teaching work all over the world.

The Job Hunter's Guide to Japan by Terra Brockman. A guide to finding work in thirteen different fields. Includes names, addresses and phone numbers of companies that hire foreigners.

Tokyo: a Bilingual Atlas. An essential part of every expat's life. Pick this up before you go and get oriented to the big city.

Webster's English—Japanese, Japanese—English pocket dictionary. This dictionary has Japanese written in roman letters and kanji.

You Gotta Have Wa by Robert Whiting. The best book I've read concerning Japanese culture. Japanese society is explained in the context of foreigners playing baseball in Japan. Even if you aren't a baseball fan, this is a must-read.

● ● ● ● ● ● ● ●

Selected book publishers

The following publishers have extensive catalogs of Japan-related titles.

Japan Times USA
Suite K105, Costa Mesa, CA 92626-4625
TEL: (714) 549-2555   FAX: (714) 549-2888

Kondansha America
114 Fifth Avenue, 18th Floor, New York, NY 10011
TEL: (212) 727-6460

Charles E. Tuttle Company, Inc.
2-6 Suido 1-chome, Bunkyo-ku, Tokyo, Japan 112

Kinokuniya bookstores

This chain of Japanese book stores has a great selection of books about Japan. You can also find the *Tokyo Journal* here.

1581 Webster St., San Francisco, CA 94115 (415) 567-7625

675 Saratoga Ave., San Jose, CA 95129 (408)252-1300

591 6th Ave. South, Seattle WA. 98104

123 Astronaut Ellison S. Onizuka St., Suite 106 Los Angeles, CA 90012 (213) 687-4480

2141 West 182nd St., Torrance, CA 90504 (301) 327-6577

401 Newport Center Dr. 315, Newport Beach, CA 92626 (714)640-1505

675 Paularino Ave., Costa Mesa, CA 92626 (714) 434-9986

10 West 49th St., New York, NY 10020 (212) 765-1461

595 River Road #B-101, Edgewater, NJ 07020 (201) 941-7580

1 Rockefeller Plaza Room #325, New York, NY 10020 (212)765-1465

Japanese embassies and consulates

Embassy of Japan

2520 Massachusetts Ave. NW, Washington D.C. 20008-2869 (202) 939-6700

Consulate General of Japan

Suite 1501, 400 Colony Square Bldg, 1201 Peachtree St. NE, Atlanta, GA 30361 (404) 892-2700

Finding the Best Jobs 165

2519 Commerce Tower, 911 Main St., Kansas, MO 64105
(816) 471-0111

50 Fremont St., Suite 2300, San Francisco, CA 94105
(415) 777-3533

601 Union St., Suite 500, Seattle, WA 98101 (206) 682-9107

Olympia Center, Suite 1100, 737 N. Michigan Ave, Chicago, IL 60611 (312) 280-0400

Suite 2050, One Poydras Plaza, 639 Loyola Ave, New Orleans, LA 70113 (504) 529-2101

299 Park Avenue, New York, NY 10017 (212) 371-8222

5300 First Interstate Bank Plaza, 1000 Louisiana St., Houston, TX77002 (713) 652-2977

2400 First Interstate Tower, 1300 SW 5th Ave., Portland, OR 97201 (503) 221-1811

Federal Reserve Plaza, 600 Atlantic Ave., Boston, MA 02210
(617) 973-9772

1742 Nuuanu Ave., Honolulu, HI 96817 (808) 536-2226

250 East First St., #1507, Los Angeles, CA 90012
(213) 624-8305

909 West 9th Ave., #301, Anchorage, AK 99501
(907) 279-8428

Embassy of Japan

255 Sussex Dr., Ottawa, Ontario K1N-9E6, Canada
(613) 236-8541

Consulate General of Japan

#900- 1177 West Hastings St., Vancouver, B.C. V6E-2K9 Canada (604) 684-5868

730-215 Garry St., Credit Union Central Plaza, Winnipeg, Manitoba R3C-3P3 (204) 943-5554, 942-7991

2480 Manulife Place, 10180-101 St., Edmonton, Alberta
T5J-3S4, Canada (403) 422-3752, 423-4750

Suite 2707, Toronto Dominion Bank Tower, P.O. Box 10,
Toronto Dominion Centre, Toronto, Ontario M5K 1A1 Canada
(416) 363-7038 Japan Information Centre: (416) 363-5488

600 rue de la Gauchetiere ouest, Suite 1785, Montreal, Quebec
H3B 4L8 Canada (514) 866-3429

Japan National Tourist Organization

360 Post Street, Suite 601, San Francisco, CA 94108
(415) 989-7140

The JNTO sends free maps, hotel listings, festival info, and other tourist information upon request.

Hyogo Cultural Center

2001 Sixth Avenue, Suite 1101, Seattle, WA 98121
(206) 728-0610

School for International Training

P.O. Box 676, Brattleboro, VT 05302 (800) 451-4465

Offers a world-known, highly respected M.A. in TESL. SIT also has program in which you can earn an M.A. while teaching in Japan.

Edmonds Community College

ECC International Division, 20000 68th Ave. West,
Lynnwood, WA (206) 771-7478

ECC has a branch campus in Kobe, Japan (near Osaka). They offer packages that include airfare, housing, and tuition at a very reasonable cost.

National Association of Japan-America Societies (NAJAS)

The Japan America Society (JAS) has great resources for anyone considering going to Japan.

JAS of Alabama Room 7N-0015, 600 North 18th St., Birmingham, AL 35291-0015 (205) 250-2077

JAS of Austin, P.O. Box 1967, Austin, TX 78767 (512) 472-0269

JAS of Boston, 22 Batterymarch St. Boston, MA 02109 (617) 451-0726

JAS of Greater Cincinnati, 300 Carew Tower, 441 Vine St., Cincinnati, OH 45202-2812 (513) 579-3114

JAS of Central Florida, P.O. Box 23744, Tampa, FL 33623 (813) 289-6283

JAS of Chicago, 303 West Madison Street, Suite 1020, Chicago, IL 60606 (312) 263-3049

JAS of Colorado, 707 Seventeenth St., Suite 2300, Denver, CO 80202 (303) 296-2323 ext.8306

JAS of Dallas, c/o Pete Marwick, Suite 1400, Thanksgiving Tower, 1601 Elm St., Dallas, TX 75201 (214) 754-2367

JAS of Georgia, Suite 710, South Tower, 225 Peachtree St. NE, Atlanta, GA 30303 (404) 524-7399

Greater Detroit and Windsor, JAS Suite 1500, 150 West Jefferson, Detroit, MI 48226 (313) 963-1988

JAS of Hawaii, P.O. Box 1412, Honolulu, HI 96806 (808) 524-4450

JAS of Houston, Suite 301, 17 S. Briar Hollow Lane, Houston, TX 77027 (713) 963-8376

JAS of Indiana, Suite 1570, First Indiana Plaza, 135 North Pennsylvania St., Indianapolis, IN 46204-2491 (317) 635-0123

JAS of Kentucky, P.O. Box 333, Lexington, KY 40584 (606) 231-7533

JAS of Maine, One Bank Road, P.O. Box 8461, Portland, ME 04104 (207) 774-4014

JAS of Minnesota, 6101 Halifax Ave South, Edina, MN 55435 (612) 920-5182

JAS of New Hampshire, P.O. Box 1226, Portsmouth, NH 03802-1226 (603) 43301360

Japan Society Inc., 333 East 47 St., New York, NY 10017 (212) 832-1155

JAS of Northern California, Suite 630, 350 Sansome St., San Francisco, CA 94104 (415) 986-4383

JAS of Oklahoma, P.O. Box 50476, Midwest City, OK 73110 (405) 670-3033

Japan-Oklahoma Society, 115 East Gray, Norman, OK 73069 (405) 360-4600

JAS of Oregon, 221 NW Second Ave, Portland, OR 97209 (503) 228-9411 ext.235,236

JAS of Phoenix, Suite 203, 10827 South 51 St., Phoenix, AZ 85044 (602) 893-0599

JAS of Pennsylvania, Suite 1614, 500 Wood St., Pittsburgh, PA 15222 (412) 281-4440

JAS of Philadelphia, c/o Blank, Rome, Comisky & McCauley, Four Penn Center Plaza, Philadelphia, PA 19103

JAS of Rhode Island, Providence, RI (401) 864-2720

JAS of San Antonio, 411 SW 24th St., San Antonio, TX 78207-4666 (512) 340-6090

JAS of Southern California, ARCO Plaza, Level C, 505 South Flower St., Los Angeles, CA 90071 (213) 627-6217

JAS of South Florida, World Trade Center, #2000, 80 SW 8th St., Miami, FL 33130 (305) 358-6006

JAS of St. Louis, 25 North Brentwood Blvd. St. Louis, MO 63105 (314) 726-6822

The Japan Canter of Tennessee, Cope Administration Bldg. Suite 218, Middle Tennessee State University, Murfreesboro, TN 37132 (615) 898-2229

JAS of Tucson, 4511 East Tenth St., Tucson, AZ 85711 (602) 881-5670

JAS of Tulsa, P.O. Box #52073, Tulsa, OK 74152 (918) 582-2456

JAS of Vermont, 92 Ethan Allen Ave. Suite 321, Fort Ethan Allen, Colchester, VT 05446 (802) 655-4197

The Japan Virginia, Society Suite 304, 803 East Main St., Richmond, VA 23219 (804) 783-0740

JAS of Washington D.C., Dacor-Bacon House Mews, 606 18th St. NW, Washington, D.C. 20006 (202) 289-8290

JAS of Washington State, One Union Square Building, Suite 2420, 600 University St., Seattle, WA 98101-3163 (206) 623-7900

JAS of Wisconsin , 424 East Wisconsin Ave., Milwaukee, WI 53202-4406 (414)272-5160

The Japan Study Group Cleveland, Council on World Affairs 539 Hanna Bldg., Cleveland, OH 44115-1901 (216)781-3730

The Japan Cultural Society of Northwest Florida, P.O. Box 11512, Pensacola, FL 32524-11512

The Japan Society, P.O. Box 183, South Tower, Royal Bank Plaza, Toronto, Ontario Canada M5J-2J4 (416) 777-0216

Budget Accomodations in Tokyo

Tokyo International Youth Hostel 3235-1107
1 minute walk from Iidabashi station on JR and subway (Tozai) lines.

Yoyogi Youth Hostel 3467-9163
10 Minutes from Sangubashi station on Odakyu line.

Kimi Ryokan 3971-3766
5 minutes from JR Ikebukuro staion (West exit).

House Ikebukuro 3984-3399
6 minutes from JR Ikebukuro station (West exit).

Shin-Nakano Lodge 3381-4886
5 minutes from Shin-Nakano station on Murunouchi line (subway).

Rikko Kaikan Guest Room 3972-1151
10 minutes from Kotake-Hukaihara station on Yurakucho line (subway).

YMCA (men and women) 3233-0611
8 minutes from Suidobashi station on JR or Toei Mita line (subway).

Tokyo YWCA 3268-4452
3 minutes from Ichigaya station on JR or subway Yurakucho and Toei Shinjuku lines.

Assume all rooms have a share toilet. They may have a share bath or they may send you to the local public bath (*sento*). To call Tokyo from the U.S., dial 011-813 then the eight digit number listed above. Always speak simply and slowly.

TOKYO HOUSING

1A HOUSE information center. Call (0422) 51-2277 Fax (0422) 43-2123. Six locations within 20 mins. from Shinjuku sta. Free job placement and picking up service. Private ¥69,000-/mo. Share ¥30,000 / mo. Weekly ¥8,400. Daily ¥2,000. etc.

2 MIN. KAMEIDO 9 min. Tokyo sta. ¥4,- 1 day, 45,/m (share), 70,-/m(D), 135,-/m(s), ladies, any svc incl. moving 3,-/h C0SMO CLUB HTS. 13 -22. 3636-3981, 24hr. Beep 5052-9021.

AFFORDABLE ADORABLE ACCOMMODATION: "TOKYO HOUSE" I AND III. [I] (3391-5577) Ogikubo, - on JR Chuo or Subway Marunouchi lines. 8 min. to Shinjuku. [III] (3910-8808) Otsuka, -conveniently located on JR Yamanote line. 3 min. to Ikebukuro, 9 min. to Shinjuku. No dep./key ¥. From ¥34,500/mo. Deal!

A FIRST CALL (3383-0975) Shinnakano Guest House newly open, convenient location near Shinjuku. 1 min. walk from Shinnakano sta. (Marunouchi line) Single ¥75,000, TW. ¥55,000. No key money.

ABBEY HOUSE (0424-23-4162) 8 mins from HIBARIGAOKA (2nd exp stop/Seibu Ikebukuro) w/ satellite TV. Single ¥42,000 up, no key/dep. Clean, cheap and friendly.

SUPER CLEAN HOUSE (3400-4900) 5 min. from Yoyogi Uehara. Very sunny, clean. Share: ¥50,000/ mo. Inc. utilities. Private ¥80,000/ mo. Inc. utilities.

ACADIA HOUSE On Chiyoda line 17 min. to Roppongi. Share ¥59,000. Call 5814-5238.

ACCOMMODATION IN PRIVILEGE Mejiro (on Yamanote line) Tabata (on Yamanote line) Akabane (on Saikyo line) Shimurasakaue (on Mita line) Tsudanuma (on Sobu line) Private; ¥40,000 ~¥90,000/mo. ¥12,000 ~ ¥20,000/week. Share; ¥30,000 ~¥60,000/mo. ¥10,000 ~¥16,000/ week. 5391-0469 or 3558-0721.

ACCOMMODATION ZEN HOUSE I Minamigyotoku/ Tozai line, fully furnished priv. rms. Musashishino/ Nanbu line. (Good for Shibuya/Yokohama/Kawasaki) 6-8 mats, priv. rms. Single ¥66,000 Double ¥73,000. Share ¥42,000. The longer you stay, the cheaper it gets. Weekly (Single ¥18,000) also available. Call (044) 755-4944.

APARTMENT-INFO We have many furnished private rooms and luxurious apartments in different locations. (03) 3748-3345.

APPLE HOUSE New Guest house. Call (0423) 877701 Fax Reservation: (0423) 86-0220. Daily, weekly, monthly available.

ARAI GUEST HOUSE (0473) 98-3370 (English), (0473) 98-3380 (Japanese) From ¥45,000/mo., ¥2000/day. Any nationality O.K. Call us for more information.

BILINGUAL HOUSE five houses on Seibu-Shinjuku Line, Keio Line and JR Line. Nice rooms with common facilities. Twin ¥33,000-¥40,000, single ¥55,000-70,000/mo. Tel 3200-7082.

COSMOPOLITAN HOUSE Y40,000 (D) ¥59,000 (P) 20 min. to Shinjuku sta. Nice, lounge & common kitchen. Call (03) 3926-4746 Akimoto.

ESTHER HOUSE Single or double rooms from ¥75,000. In Nish-Ogikubo or Ogikubo on JR Chuo Line. Quiet tenants only. Call Darron at 3398-7559.

FRIENDSHIP HOUSE 5 convenient places. Clean and nice people. 1) Higashi Koenji on Marunouchi Line.
2) Hachimanyama Keio line
3) Oimachi on JR. 4) Kichijoji on JR. 5) Shakujiikoen on Seibu line. Share ¥9200~¥10,400/week. Single ¥16,750/wk. Double ¥20,000/wk. Call 3327-3179. Information (045) 546-1163, 3314-7441.

GAIJIN GUEST HOUSES: All in Tokyo only ¥20,000 deposit, various arrangements from ¥45,000 to ¥110,000. Utilities included. Call Sakura House (03) 3408-1661.

HIGASHI NAKANO ENGLISH CENTER (3360-1666, 4781) (JR Sobu Line). Very convenient location, center of Tokyo, two stops from Shinjuku sta., 3 min. walk from the JR & subway sta. Share room ¥1900/ day, ¥47,000/mo. No key money. All facilities.

JAPAN HOUSE Convenient location, new: lounge, shower, kitchen, TV etc. Monthly rent from ¥42,000. Kamata Sta. (Keihin Tohoku Line). 3962-2495, 37397925. Ask for Arold.

KIWI APARTMENTS Why don't you live in your own furnished apartment in price almost like a guest house. We have different locations. No key money also guest house available with private & shared rooms. All nationalities welcome. Call (045) **564 3417,** Fax (045) **5643797.**

LIBERTY HOUSE (5272-7238) New opened very clean building w/AC, TV, VCR. 7 min. to Shinjuku & Ikebukuro. 5 min. walk Waseda sta. Shared ¥29,000 /mo.~¥9,000 /w.Private ¥49,000 /mo. ¥14,000 /w. No key money.

LILY HOUSE MANSION: Sunny, clean, quiet, furnished, convenient. Kawaguchi sta. Keihin Tohoku line. No deposit. Share: ¥50,000/Pri.: ¥70,000. (0482) 23-8205.

LUXURIOUS Rooms in Apts or Houses (1 to 6 people per house). Fully furnished, TV, video, etc... Locations: Nakano (JR) and Shinjuku. Share: ¥53,000. Single: ¥70,000. TEL: 5385-6720, (030) 223-6622 (anytime).

AT MAHARJAH-PLACE (03-3728-7061/54993779) Very clean. Video-Salon, reading-room and big garden. Convenient location 12 min. to Gotanda, 30 min. to Shibuya. From ¥59,000/mo. (single), ¥70,000/mo. (double), ¥9,000/weekly (shared).

MIDORI HOUSE (3754-3112) Longterm only (6 month minimum) Grouphouse, ¥51,000/mo.(s) or ¥85,000/mo.(d) No key money/deposit, call taken 8-10pm, better, Nishimagome sta. Call.

MOMS HOUSE Hiroo, Harajuku and other excellent locationsl ¥55,000~¥60,000 per mo. No key money. 5410-4005 ask for Mike or call 5568-0123 ask for Tsuneo.

SAKURA SLEEP INN ASAKUSA Reservation office (03) 5330-5250 office hours 9am-6pm. One day per person: ¥1500. Address: 2-21-1, Asakusa Taitoku, Tokyo, Japan. Dormitory type room with kitchen/ W.C.

SHARE ROOMS located 15 min. walk from JR Omori (2 stops from Shinagawa), accommodated with bath room, kitchen, air conditioners, TV ¥4,000/day or ¥53,000 ~¥60,000/mo. Tel: 3763-4839 (daytime & weekend) 3574-6126 (6-12p.m.).

SHIMOKITAZAWA HOUSE 3780-2611. ¥45,000~¥85,000/mo. Only for 1-11/mo. One mo. key money. One mo. refunded deposit. 10 min. walk from Setagayadaita sta. (Odakyu line) Nice & Quiet location. Call to us Nihon M.K.D.

TAIHEI HOUSE No. 0 (3940-4705) Responsible owner, also fine room from Komagome JR line 30 min. to downtown. ¥30,000/mo. Double: ¥35,000 single: ¥55,000. No key money.

TOKYO ENGLISH CENTER Fujimigaoka sta. (Keio Inokashira Line) Share Room ¥2,000/day ¥52,000/ mo. No Key Money. All Facilities. Air Condition. Tel: 5370-8440. Cellular: 030-570-0692.. Car for Greeting & Farewell (Narita-Tokyo) ¥14,000. For Moving ¥3,000/hour.

TOYAMA HOUSE (0422-49-8938) We're looking for good people to rent our rooms. Several good rooms available. In pleasant surroundings. Ogikubo & Nakano, serious people only need apply.

VILLA PARADIS0 (045-911-1184) clean, quiet, big kitchen, common room. 20 min. to Shibuya or Yokohama. Tama plaza sta. Shintamagawa line. ¥64,000 ¥66,000 single/month free shower.

YOKOHAMA HILLSTONE HOUSE (045-243-3210) Exciting location, 2 common kitchens, clean, convenient, share or private room ¥45,000~¥75,000/mo. Maintenance fee ¥3,000. Good people welcome.

YTC HOUSE (3946-5266 & 3942-2887) Near Sugamo station (JR Yamanote line). Share room, ¥45,000/mo. air conditioned, TV, Tel, refrigerator, bath, flush toilet, wash machine, no key money.

ZEN HOUSE Minamigyotoku/Tozai line, fully furnished (TV, VCR, A/C, refrig. etc) Priv. rms. 6-8mats ¥83,000. Call 0473-58-4926.

APARTMENT 8 min. Nakamurabashi St. Seibu-Ikebukuro line. 3 rooms inside for 1-5 persons, ¥145,000-¥165,000/mo. deposit, utilities necessary, call 3313-6236.

APARTMENT TEACHER'S VILLAGE, 3327-3179. (045) 546-1163. 1) Itabashi Honcho sta. on Mita line. Room with kitchen and phone. 2) Shakujii koen sta. Seibu Ikebukuro line. Nice people & clean. Double or single ¥20,000/w, ¥86,000/mon.

APT AND MANSION fully furnished: AC/Heating, phone, refrigerator, bilingual TV-Video/satellite, washing machine, cleaner, carpet bedding set, an iron set, kitchen set, microwave etc. 30 min. to Ginza, Gyotoku sta. on Tozai line. ¥62,000-¥75,000 (Private), ¥87,000 ¥107,000 (1 bedroom), ¥125000-¥148,000 (2 bedroom), ¥201,000 ¥210,000 (3 bedroom), total 180 RMs. No key money. Arai housing Co., Ltd. Tel. (0473) 98-3370 (English), (0473) 98-3380 (Japanese).

EIFUKU HOUSE (3780-2611) ¥50,000~¥100,000/mo. Only for 1~11mo. One mo. key mo/Dep. 1 min. walk from Nishi-Eifuku sta. (Inokashira line) We're sure you'll like it!! For more information Nihon M.K.D.

FURNISHED APARTMENTS Gyotoku on Tozai Line. No key money, one month deposit. ¥65,000. includ. utilities. Single room w/shared DK and bathroom. CHITOSE CO. (03) 3561-1122.

FURNISHED APARTMENTS FOR RENT. Harajuku, Shibuya, Roppongi, Central Tokyo. From ¥80,000 ~¥200,000. No key money. Only one month deposit. Call now 3400-4990

INTERNATIONAL GUEST HOUSE (3266-0979) several locations. Share room ¥40,000 ~¥50,000. Private room ¥60,000 ¥70,000. Apartment with loft ¥88,000~¥110,000. All furnished, clean, no key money.

MARUI HOUSE (3962-4979) 5 min. walk from Ikebukuro JR Sta. West exit. Single ¥50,000/mo. Shared ¥43,000/mo. Quiet & very clean room available. Also in Shin-Okubo (JR) located in central Tokyo.

PRIVATE FURNISHED ROOMS from ¥51,000/mo. No key money. One mo. refunded deposit. Gyotoku Station, Tozai Line, 30 minutes subway to Ginza. (0473) 96-0715.

ROOM FOR RENT IN NEW 3LDK APARTMENT Only girls (for 2G). ~¥20,000 deposit. Furnished and all elec. appliances included. Gas and electric bills included in rent. One person-¥50,000. 10 min. from J.R. Koiwa Sta. Call: Hoshino 3602-4823 (day time). 3844-4341 (19:00 pm- 24:00)

STUDIO APTS ALSO HOUSE SHARE dormitory rooms or studio apartment at Ekota-Seibu Ikebukuro line ¥40,000-¥80,000 per month. Tel: 3955-0829 No key money.

TOKYO HOUSE BUREAU (3501-2496) 1 min. from Toranomon Sta. Rental houses or apartments, Tokyo, Yokohama and suburban areas. Long established and most experienced real estate agency.

The Daily Yomiuri

The Daily Yomiuri is a morning, English language newspaper. Classified ads appear on Sunday and Monday. Although the *help wanted* section is practically useless, the rest of the classifieds are great. Ads can be placed in the paper *for free*. It's an excellent place to find second-hand furnishings, bikes etc. People also advertise for volleyball teams, housemates, sublets, etc.

About once a month there is a free movie ticket give-away in the paper. Just send in a postcard and you'll receive a pass good for two people to see a new movie.

Every Thursday there an education page with articles by various people about education around Japan.

The problem is this paper can be hard to find. Not all kiosks carry this paper and the ones that do only carry a few copies. You can subscribe for only ¥1,550 per month.

To order call 03-3216-8866

Pia magazine and guides

Pia is one of the largest entertainment companies in Japan. They do just about everything within the industry. They publish a number of bilingual entertainment guides for restaurants, bars, concert halls and more. *Tokyo Knock-out* is an English/Japanese guide book containing a large variety of things to do in Tokyo.

Pia Magazine is a weekly entertainment magazine that lists movie times, concert schedules, sports events, gallery showings, TV programs, etc. Because it is written in Japanese only, most foreigners don't even try to use it. Actually it is quite easy to use if you can read Katakana and a few kanji. You can also find entertainment listings in the *Tokyo Journal* and other English magazines, but their listings are grossly incomplete. Concerts are usually listed too late to get tickets.

If you want to order tickets, it can be done by calling ticket Pia. Just tell them what show you want to see, your name, and phone number. You then have a week to go to a Pia office to pick up and pay for the tickets. If you want to conduct this transaction in English, just say *Eigo hanashitain deskedo.* They will connect you to someone who speaks English.

Immigration forms

CERTIFICATE OF ELIGIBILITY

日本国政府法務省
Ministry of Justice, Japanese Government

番　号
No.

氏　名 Name　Family Name	Given Name	性別　男　女 Sex　M　F	写真　photo 40mm×30mm
国　籍 Nationality	生年月日 Date of Birth	年　月　日 Year Month Day	

日本での職業及び勤務(通学)先等
Profession or Occupation/Organization to be employed or to study in Japan

上記の者は、次の在留資格に関して出入国管理及び難民認定法第七条第一項第二号に掲げる上陸のための条件に適合していることを証明する。
Under the following status, it is hereby certified that the above-mentioned person meets requirement for the landing provided in Article 7, Paragraph 1, Item 2 of the Immigration-Control and Refugee Recognition Act.

在留資格
Status   (   )

　　　　年　　月　　日
　　　　Year　Month　Day
Date
　　　　法務大臣に代わり
　　　　For Minister of Justice

(注意)　Notice
1　本証明書は、上陸の申請の際に入国審査官に提出しなければならない。
　　This certificate should be submitted to an Immigration Inspector to apply for the landing permission at a port of entry.
2　本証明書は、上記の年月日から3ヵ月以内に上陸の申請を行わないときは、効力を失う。
　　This Certificate shall cease to be valid if the application for landing permisson is not filed within 3 months from the date of issue.
3　本証明書は、上陸許可を保証するものではない。他の上陸のための条件に適合しない場合又は事情の変更があった場合は上陸を許可されないことがある。
　　This Certificate does not guarantee the entry of the person concerned.
　　In case that the applicant does not fulfill other requirements for the landing or the relevant circumstances are found to be changed, the landing permission would be denied.

別記第三十号様式(第二十条関係)
その1
PART 1

Ministry of Justice, Japanese Government

在留資格変更許可申請書
APPLICATION FOR CHANGE OF STATUS OF RESIDENCE

To the Minister of Justice

1. Nationality: **U.S.A.**
2. Family Name: **Mcdonald** Given Names: **Elizabeth**
3. Sex: Male / (Female)
4. Date of Birth: **1968** Year **9** Month **23** Day
5. Place of Birth: **New York**
6. Marital Status: Married / (Single)
7. Occupation: **Student**
8. Address in Home Country: **140 E. 46 St. N.Y.**
9. Address in Japan: **3-3-20 Konandoi Shinagawa-ku** Telephone No: **(3123) 4565**
10. Passport (1) Number: **U-7891011** (2) Date of Issue: **1985** Year **3** Month **2** Day
    (3) Date of Expiration: **1992** Year **3** Month **1** Day (4) Issuing Authority: **Department of State**
11. Date of Entry (Residence) Permit: **1987** Year **3** Month **3** Day
12. Port of Entry: **Narita**
13. Status of Residence: **留学** Period of Stay: **1 year** Date of Expiration: **1991** Year **3** Month **3** Day
14. Alien Registration Certificate Number: **⑬ 121314**
15. Embarkation Card Number: **AB 161715**
16. New Status Desired: **技術** Desired Period of Stay: **1 year**
17. Reason for Change of Status of Residence: **To work at Showa Electric Industrial Co., LTD.**

18. Family in Japan (Father, Mother, Spouse, Son, Daughter)

Relationship	Name	Age	Nationality	Residing with Applicant or Not	Occupation	Status of Residence / Period of Stay
			NIL			

(注) 様式その2にも記載して下さい。裏面参照。 Note Followed by Form Part 2. See Notes on Reverse Side

官　用　欄　FOR OFFICIAL USE ONLY

別記第30号の2様式 第二十一条関係
その1
PART 1

Ministry of Justice, Japanese Government

在留期間更新許可申請書
APPLICATION FOR EXTENSION OF PERIOD OF STAY

法務大臣殿
To the Minister of Justice

1. 国籍 Nationality: **U.S.A.**
2. 氏名 Name — Family Name: **Mcdonald**, Given Names: **Elizabeth, P.**
3. 性別 Sex: Male / **Female**
4. 生年月日 Date of Birth: **1963** Year **9** Month **23** Day
5. 出生地 Place of Birth: **New York**
6. 配偶者の有無 Marital Status: Married / **Single**
7. 職業 Occupation: **English Teacher**
8. 本国における居住地 Address in Home Country: **N.Y. city U.S.A.**
9. 日本における居住地 Address in Japan: **3-3-20 Konandai, Shinagawa-ku, Tokyo c/o Mr. Hachiro Yamamoto** 電話番号 Telephone No. **123-4567**
10. 旅券番号 Passport Number: **B-345678** (2) 発行年月日 Date of Issue: **1985** Year **3** Month **2** Day
    (3) 有効期限 Date of Expiration: **1995** Year **3** Month **1** Day (4) 発行機関 Issuing Authority: **State Department**
11. 上陸年月日 Date of Entry / Residence Permit: **1991** Year **3** Month **20** Day
12. 上陸港 Port of Entry: **Narita**
13. 現に有する在留資格 Status of Residence: **教育** 在留期間 Period of Stay: **1 year** 在留期間満了日 Date of Expiration: **1992** Year **3** Month **20** Day
14. 外国人登録証明書番号 Alien Registration Certificate Number: **⑭ 3456789**
15. 出入国記録番号 Embarkation Card Number: **AB1234567**
16. 希望する在留期間 Desired Length of Extension: **1 year**
17. 更新の理由 Reason for Extension: **To continue work as English teacher**
18. 在日家族 父・母・配偶者・子 Family in Japan: Father, Mother, Spouse, Son, Daughter

続柄 Relationship	氏名 Name	年齢 Age	国籍 Nationality	同居の有無 Residing with Applicant or Not	職業 Occupation	在留資格・在留期間 Status of Residence Period of Stay
			none			

(注) 様式その2にも記載して下さい。裏面参照。 Note: Followed by Form Part 2. See Notes on Reverse Side.

官用欄 FOR OFFICIAL USE ONLY

(注) 別記第30号の2様式その2 B、C、D、E 及び第34号様式その2は、入管窓口でまだ改正前の様式が使用されているため旧様式で示しました。

Finding the Best Jobs

PART 2 B (BUSINESS, EMPLOYMENT)

19. Type of Work
- [ ] a Management
- [ ] b Marketing
- [ ] c Translation, Interpretation, Copywriting
- [ ] d Overseas Business
- [ ] e Design
- [ ] f Public Relations
- [ ] g Research
- [ ] h Technical Development
- [ ] i Data Processing
- [ ] j Trade
- [ ] k International Finance
- [ ] l Legal Services
- [ ] m Accounting
- [x] n Education
- [ ] o Journalism
- [ ] p Cooking
- [ ] q Medical Services
- [ ] r Other

20. Term of Employment Contract: **1 year**
21. Monthly Salary: **250,000** Yen
22. Position: **none**

23. Place of Employment
(1) Name: **ABC English Language School** Established Year: **1970, 4, 1**

(3) Type of Business:
- A Manufacturing: a Machinery, b Electrical, c Telecommunications, d Automobil, e Steel, f Chemicals, g Textiles, h Other
- B Transportation: a Airline, b Shipping, c Travel Agency, d Other
- C Finance: a Banking, b Insurance, c Security, d Other
- D Commerce: a Trade, b Department Store, c Other
- E Education: a University, b Senior High School, [x] c Language School, d Other
- F Journalism: a News, b Newspaper, c Broadcasting, d Other
- G Professional: a Attorneys, b Certified Accountant, c Patent Attorney, d Other
- H Construction / I Computer Services / J Dispatch of Personnel / K Advertising / L Hotel / M Restaurant
- N Medical Services / O Publishing / P Research / Q Other

(4) Address: **1-3-1 Ote-machi, Chiyoda-ku, Tokyo** Telephone No. **123-4567**
(5) Capital: **50,000,000** Yen (6) Ratio of Foreign Capital: ___% (7) Annual Sales: **500,000,000** Yen
(8) Amount of Corporate Income Tax: **2,000,000** Yen (9) Amount of Consumption Tax for Meal To be Filled in by Cook, etc Only: ___ Yen
(10) Number of Employees: **135** (11) Number of Foreign Members: **100**

24. Organization Sending Applicant
(1) Name: ___
(2) Address: ___
(3) Type of Business: ___ (4) Capital: ___ (5) Annual Sales: ___

25. Education Last School or Institution: **U.C.L.A.** Field of Specialization: **English literature**

26. Professional Experience

Year	Month	Employment History	Year	Month	Employment History
1989	6	Graduated U.C.L.A.			
1989	7	Employed by ABC high school			
1991	1	Resigned from ABC high school			

27. Guarantor or Contact in Japan
(1) Name: **Saburo Suzuki**
(2) Address: **1-3-1 Ote-machi, Chiyoda-ku, Tokyo** Telephone No. **123-4567**

Signature of Applicant: *Elizabeth D. Mc* Year **1991** Month **4** Day **10**

FOR OFFICIAL USE ONLY

Useful phone numbers: Tokyo

Police	110
Fire and Ambulance	119
Hospital Information	3212-2323
American Pharmacy	3271-4034
International telephone assistance	0051
Tokyo English Life Line (TELL)	3264-4347
Foreign Resident Advisory Center	3211-4433
Kimi Information Service	3986-1604
Immigration	3213-8111
	3471-0031
Tourist Information	3277-1010
JR Infoline	3423-0111
Bicycle Culture Center	3584-4530
Airport Baggage Service (ABC)	3545-1131
Department of Motor Vehicles	474-1374 ext 271

Index

Abbreviations 72
Accommodations 36
Adult classes 46
Age 10
Air tickets 37
Airfare 23
Alien registration 111
Answering services 44
Apartments 24
Assistant English teachers 48
ATM cards 121

Baggage 43
Bank accounts 36
Banking 121
Benefits 64
Bonuses 60, 61
Budget 120

Canceled lessons 60
Changing sponsors 114
Changing visa status 31
Class size 58
Classified ads 70
Clothes 38, 84
Cold calling 78
College Degree 9, 15, 37
Company classes 50
Completion bonus 60
Contracts 24, 96, 97
Cultural visas 32
Culture shock 134-137

Daily Yomiuri 176
Demand for teachers 14
Dispatch companies 52

Economy 7
Educators 9
English Conversation
    schools 46
English in Japan 11, 13
English teachers 81
Evaluating students 151
Expenses 17
Experience 34

Finding a Doctor 123
Finding an Apartment 114
Fukuoka 29

Gender 10
Getting around 80

Health care 122
Hiragana 132
Hiring cycles 22
Hiring in Japan 24,25
Hiring in US 23
Hotels 170
Hours 70
Housing 51, 171-175

Immigration 108
Immigration forms 178-181
International driver's license
    38
Interviews 91-95

Japan Times 29, 71
Japan tourist information 43
Japan/America Societies 167
Japanese companies 160
Japanese consulates 165
Japanese Embassies 164
Japanese Language
  16, 28, 35, 123
Japanese language schools
  130
Jr and Sr high schools
  48, 149

Kanji 126
Katakana 133
Key money 118
Kimi Information Center
  44, 45
Kinokuniya Bookstores 164

Lesson planning 142
Letter of release 93
Location, job 24, 57

Mail 44
Misc visas 33
Miscellaneous teaching work
  54
Money 35, 120

Narita airport 42
National Health Insurance
  122
Negotiating 97
Non-teaching jobs 159

Offers 87, 96
Office services 44
Osaka 29

Packing 39, 40
Paperwork 37
Pay 15, 24, 60, 61, 63, 66
Preparation, long term 33
Phone numbers 182
Pia 176
Population 13
Private lessons 53, 152
Private language schools 46
Problems in the classroom
  154

Qualifications 15, 17
Quitting 24, 105

Race 82
Racism 19
Re-entry permits 108
Recommended reading 162
Requirements 71
Resumes 90, 91

Safety 7
Sample lessons 145, 146
Sapporo 29
Schedules 56, 71
Schedules, samples 62, 64
School year 22
Sick pay 61
Split schedules 71
Sponsors 31
Sponsorship 59
Students 58

Teaching 140
Teaching adults 148
Teaching children 151
Teaching materials
        57, 152-153
Team- teaching 48
Telephone, using 79
Telephone, service 119
Temporary housing 95, 171
Tokyo
        Apartments 28
        Employment 26, 27
        Getting to 42
        Living conditions 28
        Phone numbers 182
Tourist information 43
Tourist visas 30, 72
Training 34, 57

Universities 54

Visas 18, 23
Visas 30
Vocational schools 51

Weather 38
What to take 40
When to go 22
Work conditions 63, 65
Working visas 31

Yen rate 3

About the author

Douglas McNamee moved to Tokyo in 1987 after graduating from the University of Washington with a degree in Broadcast Journalism. Douglas promotes travel in Japan through seminars, slide shows, and related consulting. Between seminars Douglas takes pictures for various publications in Japan and the U.S., and works with ESL students at the University of Washington.

Order Information

To order a copy of this book please send a check for $12 plus $2 shipping and handling to:

East Asia Press
1715 NE Naomi Pl
Seattle, WA 98115
(206) 525-3646